Schlösser und Burgen
in Deutschland aus der Luft

Schlösser und Burgen in Deutschland aus der Luft

fotografiert von Dirk Laubner

Palaces and Castles in Germany from a Bird's-Eye View

Photographs by Dirk Laubner

nicolai

Inhalt

Deutsche Burgen und Schlösser aus der Vogelperspektive

Es war vor allem das Rheintal mit seinen pittoresken Burgen in erhabener Landschaft, das im 19. Jahrhundert romantische Touristen nach Deutschland zog. Bis heute sind es nicht zuletzt die ungezählten Schloss- und Burganlagen zwischen Flensburg und der Zugspitze, die alljährlich Millionen von Gästen aus aller Welt nach Deutschland locken. In besonderem Maße und auf besondere Weise sind die deutschen Städte und Landstriche von ihren Schloss- und Burgbauten geprägt. Und bei aller Unterschiedlichkeit der Landschaften und Mentalitäten gilt das für alle Bundesländer und Regionen.

Da sind die zahlreichen Residenzstädte des bis ins 19. Jahrhundert in viele kleine Fürstentümer zersplitterten Landes. In manchen von ihnen ragen alte Burgen aus den Ortskernen, vielfach prägen barocke Drei- und Vierflügelbauten die Anlage der ganzen Stadt. Da sind die mittelalterlichen Höhenburgen und ihre Nachfolger aus dem 19. Jahrhundert. Und da sind die kleinen und die großen Landsitze, die seit dem 17. Jahrhundert untrennbar mit den dazugehörigen Parkanlagen verbunden sind.

Keine Perspektive bringt diese baulichen und historischen Höhepunkte der deutschen Kulturgeschichte so sehr zum Sprechen wie die Vogelperspektive. Der Flug über Deutschlands Schlösser und Burgen sagt mehr über das Land, als sich auf der Erde erfahren lässt. Manchmal ist es die schiere Ausdehnung einer Anlage, die überrascht, manchmal die architektonische Form oder die offensichtliche Überformung in späteren Zeiten. Oft erschließt sich die Gestaltung des Bauwerks und der Parks, Gärten, Landschaften und Orte, die es umgeben, erst von oben. Und manche Großbauten wie die Wartburg oder die Burg Hohenzollern, das Heidelberger Schloss oder auch Schloss Neuschwanstein stehen wie märchenhafte Monolithen inmitten der Landschaften, die sie beherrschen, und erzählen eine Geschichte, deren Faszination sich kein Betrachter entziehen kann.

Fast immer erweisen sich Burgen und Schlösser als Keimzellen der kulturellen Erschließung ihres Umfelds. Erst aus der Luft erkennen wir, wie sie regelrecht in den Raum ausgreifen, sei es der Stadtraum oder sei es die Natur – jeweils den ästhetischen und technischen Möglichkeiten ihrer Epoche entsprechend.

Die älteren Bauten verraten aus der Luft häufig viel von ihrer Geschichte, wenn sich etwa in den Burgmauern zahlreiche Gebäudeteile aus verschiedenen Jahrhunderten zusammendrängen, während das Ganze durch mächtige, wehrhafte Mauern von der Umgebung abgeschottet wird: Schließlich waren Burgen die längste Zeit ihres Bestehens vor allem Wehrbauten, die militärischen Bedürfnissen gehorchten und deren Entwicklung viel über die Kriegsgeschichte in den deutschen Landen aussagt.

Viele Anlagen des Barock waren aus der Vogelperspektive geplant und wurden auch in zeitgenössischen Abbildungen so dargestellt. Erst die moderne Flugtechnik erlaubt es uns indes, sie auch wirklich so zu sehen. Dabei entfalten sie nicht nur ihre volle Pracht, sondern stets auch höchst individuellen Charakter, der ihre jeweilige Umgebung prägt.

Und die Anlagen des 19. und frühen 20. Jahrhunderts schließlich geben, aus der Luft betrachtet, jenes romantische Gefühl für die Landschaft zu erkennen, das die frühen Deutschlandtouristen ins Rheintal reisen ließ, das dann aber bald überall im Land in der Gestaltung und Verschönerung adeliger Landsitze allgemeine Verbreitung fand.

Dirk Laubners nord-südlicher Flug über Deutschlands Burgen und Schlösser ist eine Zeitreise und eine Baugeschichte, eine Kulturhistorie und ein ästhetischer Genuss zugleich. Die besondere Kunst besteht darin, die Distanz des Fliegenden dazu zu nutzen, uns das Gezeigte vertrauter zu machen. Kein Sujet scheint die Darstellung aus der Luft so zu suchen und zu brauchen wie die Burg- und Schlossanlagen – und das gerade in Deutschland, weil hier aufgrund der geographischen wie der historischen Situation eine so beeindruckende Vielfalt der Bautypen und Stile herrscht.

Castles and Palaces from a Bird's-Eye View

Above all, it was the Rhine River Valley, with its picturesque castles and sublime landscape that attracted Romantic Period tourists to Germany in the 19th century. Even today the numerous castles and palaces between Flensburg and the Zugspitze attract millions of visitors from the entire world each year. German cities and regions are shaped in unique ways to a great degree by their palaces and castles. Despite the differences in landscapes and mentalities throughout Germany, this is a common ground shared by all provinces and regions.

There are the numerous seats of power of a nation, which had been divided into many tiny princedoms into the 19th century. In some of them, old castles mark the 'capitols' of the cities. Many three- and four-winged constructions of the baroque period shape the identity of the entire city. And there are the medieval castles situated at great elevation and their successors of the 19th century. There are the compact and the expansive country estates, which since the 17th century have been inseparably associated with their corresponding parks and landscape gardens.

There is no other perspective like the bird's-eye view that can reveal these structural and historical climaxes of German cultural history. The flight over Germany's palaces and castles says more about the land than what can be experienced on the ground. Sometimes it is the sheer expansiveness of a construction which surprises, sometimes the architectural form or the obvious covering over of the architecture of earlier times. Often the shape of a structure opens up into the encircling parks, gardens, landscape, or area first from above. Many large structures such as Wartburg or the Castle Hohenzollern, the Heidelberg Castle or even Palace Neuschwanstein stand like monoliths from fairytales in the center of the landscape that they dominate and tell a story so fascinating that no observer can elude it.

Nearly always castles and palaces prove themselves to be foundational to cultural development in their surroundings. It is from the air that we recognize how they properly open up into space, whether it is the city or nature – always in the appropriate aesthetic and technical possibilities of the epoch.

When viewed from above, old structures reveal much of their histories. There is something in the multiple building portions from differing centuries when they huddle together in the limits of a castle's wall. While making the entire structure mighty, fortifying walls cut it off from its surroundings. For the majority of their existence, castles were above all, military structures, which were subject to the demands of battles, and whose development explains much about the history of war in German lands.

Many estates of the baroque period were planned with the bird's-eye-view in mind and were portrayed as such in contemporary drawings. Modern flight technology allows us to actually view them this way. They display not only their full majesty, but also the highly individual character offered by each of their unique settings.

The estates of the 19th and 20th centuries, when observed from above, produce every romantic feeling to be felt toward the landscape. These are the same feelings that the early tourists to Germany's Rhineland felt, which are to be found throughout the land in the structure and adornment of aristocratic country estates.

Dirk Laubner's north to south flight over Germany's castles and palaces is time-travel, building history, cultural history, and an aesthetic pleasure all at the same time. The special artistry lies in the fact that the distance is used to make us more familiar with the viewed object. No other subjects appear to call for an aerial view in their portrayal as these castles and palaces. This is especially true in Germany because of the impressive diversity of building types and style governed by geographical as well as historical circumstances.

Schlösser und Burgen
Palaces and Castles

Schloss Glücksburg

Glücksburg, Schleswig-Holstein

Eines der wichtigsten Residenzschlösser Schleswig-Holsteins ist Schloss Glücksburg, das auch als „Wiege der Europäischen Königshäuser" bekannt ist. Das Wasserschloss wurde in der Spätrenaissance – zwischen 1582 und 1587 – erbaut und war Sitz der Herzöge von Glücksburg, bis es 1779 durch das Aussterben des ältesten Familienzweigs an das dänische Königshaus fiel. 1825 erhielt Wilhelm von Schleswig-Holstein-Sonderburg-Beck das Schloss samt Herzogtitel. Aus dieser Linie ging der dänische König Christian IX. hervor, dessen Nachkommen sich wiederum in allen fürstlichen Familien Europas finden. Die charakteristische dreischiffige Anlage auf quadratischem Grundriss mit Ecktürmen, Vorburg und landseitigem Schlossgarten ist heute eine private Stiftung und kann besichtigt werden.

One of the most important residential palaces of Schleswig-Holstein is the palace of Glücksburg, which is known as 'The Cradle of the European King's Houses'. This moated castle was built in the late renaissance, between 1582 and 1587 and was the seat of the Dukes of Glücksburg until it fell into the House of the Danish King through the end of the family line in 1779. In 1825 the palace as well as the title of duke were bestowed upon Wilhelm von Schleswig-Holstein-Sonderburg-Beck. Danish King Christian IX arose out of this family line, and it is his offspring, which can be found spread throughout all of the princely families of Europe. The characteristic construction with three naves on a square ground plan, corner towers, a courtyard for economic purposes and a landward palace garden is owned by a private endowment and can be visited.

Schloss Gottorf

Gottorf bei Schleswig

Bereits im 13. Jahrhundert fand Schloss Gottorf erstmals als Bischofssitz Erwähnung. Ende des 17. Jahrhunderts wurde die vierflügelige Festungsanlage von dem schwedischen Baumeister Nicodemus Tessin für Herzog Friedrich IV. barock umgestaltet und erweitert. Der Südflügel, zur Hauptfassade ausgebaut, erhielt eine symmetrische Barockfassade. 1713 kam ein Teil der Ausstattung durch das dänische Königshaus nach Kopenhagen. Schloss Gottorf wurde noch bis 1848 vom dänischen Statthalter bewohnt. Bis Mitte des 20. Jahrhunderts wurde es als Kaserne genutzt. Seit der Nachkriegszeit ist hier das Schleswig-Holsteinische Landesmuseum untergebracht. Der im 17. Jahrhundert im Stil römischer Terrassengärten angelegte barocke Neuwerk-Garten ist bis 2007 rekonstruiert worden.

The palace of Gottorf was first mentioned as the bishop's seat in a diocesan town in the 13th century. Duke Friedrich IV commissioned the Swedish master builder Nicodemus Tessin to transfigure and enlarge the four-wing fortress structure at the end of the 17th century in the baroque style. The south-wing became the central corps de logis and received a symmetrical baroque façade. In 1713 parts of the furnishings were taken to Copenhagen by the Danish royal family. A Danish proconsul lived in the palace of Gottorf until 1848. Until the middle of the 20th century it was used as barracks. Since then it houses the famous Regional Museum of Schleswig-Holstein. The adjoined baroque Neuwerk-garden in the style of a Roman terrace garden has been reconstructed until 2007.

Gut Emkendorf

Emkendorf, Kreis Rendsburg-Eckernförde

Das Gut Emkendorf liegt südöstlich von Rendsburg in einer hügeligen, wald- und seen-reichen Landschaft. Zur Zeit des Grafen Friedrich Karl Reventlow und seiner Gattin Julia war Emkendorf im ausgehenden 18. Jahrhundert eines der Zentren des geistigen und künstlerischen Lebens nördlich der Elbe. Der Dichter Matthias Claudius hat hier das bekannte Abendlied „Der Mond ist aufgegangen" verfasst. Ab 1794 ließ Reventlow das alte barocke Herrenhaus durch den Architekten Carl Gottlob Horn außen und innen im früh-klassizistischen Stil umbauen und von dem Maler Giuseppe Anselmo Pellicia und dem Stukkateur Francesco Antonio Tadey ausgestalten. Sie gaben dem Haus die heutige Gestalt. Das Gut liegt am Hasensee und hat einen weitläufigen Landschaftspark. Das umfassend restaurierte Herrenhaus, bis 1929 Eigentum der Reventlows, ist in Privatbesitz.

Emkendorf Manor is situated in a landscape full of hills, forests, and lakes southeast of Rendsburg. At the close of the 18th century under Count Friedrich Karl Reventlow and his wife, Julia, it was one of the intellectual and artistic centers north of the Elbe. This is where poet Matthias Claudius composed the well known evening song 'Der Mond ist aufgegangen' ('The Moon Has Risen'). After 1794 Reventlow hired architect Carl Gottlob Horn to reno-vate the old baroque hall both inside and outside into an early-classicist style. Painter Giuseppe Anselmo Pellicia and plasterer Francesco Antonio Tadey are responsible for embellishments, which give the hall its current look. The manor lies on Hasensee and has an extensive scenic park. The hall was in the possession of the Reventlow family until 1929, has been restored and now remains private property.

Blomenburg

Selent, Kreis Plön

Die Blomenburg in Selent wurde als Jagdschloss nach den Plänen des Berliner Architekten und Schinkel-Schülers Eduard Knoblauch erbaut. 1927 verkaufte die gräfliche Familie Blome die Blomenburg an die Provinz Schleswig-Holstein, die hier ein Heim für Jugendliche einrichtete. Im Zweiten Weltkrieg war in der Blomenburg eine Sanitätseinheit der Deutschen Wehrmacht untergebracht, das Schlösschen wurde Aufnahmeort für zahlreiche Kriegsflüchtlinge. Das Anwesen diente nach dem Krieg wiederum als Landjugendheim, später als Übergangswohnheim. Im Zuge der Privatisierung 1993 wurde die Anlage grundlegend restauriert und durch einen Neubau nach Plänen des Hamburger Architekten Bernhard Winking ergänzt. 2006 wurde die Blomenburg als Technologiezentrum und Venturepark wiedereröffnet.

The Blomenburg, nearby the small town of Selent was built from designs by Berlin architect, Eduard Knoblauch, one of the followers of famous Karl Friedrich Schinkel. The comital family Blome sold the Blomenburg to the state of Schleswig-Holstein in 1927. Then a home for youth was established. During the Second World War, search and rescue unit for the German military was housed there, later the palace served as a home for numerous refugees. After the war, the Blomenburg again was used as a rural home for youth, and later as a transitional home. After privatization in 1993, the estate was restored and expanded through an addition designed by architect Bernhard Winking of Hamburg. The estate was re-opened as a technology center and venture park in 2006.

Schloss Plön

Plön, Schleswig-Holstein

Das Plöner Schloss ließ Herzog Johann Ernst von Schleswig-Holstein-Sonderburg-Plön von 1633 bis 1636 als mächtigen Renaissancebau errichten. Die Anlage ist ein dreiflügeliger Ziegelbau, der Ehrenhof öffnet sich zum Großen Plöner See. Der Schlosspark wurde von Georg Dietrich Tschierske im barocken Stil angelegt und im 19. Jahrhundert in einen englischen Landschaftsgarten umgestaltet. 1761 ging das Schloss in den Besitz des dänischen Königshauses über, nach 1867 fiel es der Provinz Schleswig-Holstein zu. Von der Kaiserzeit bis 1920 war das Plöner Schloss preußische Kadettenanstalt, in der Weimarer Republik staatliche Bildungsanstalt. Ab 1933 wurde es zu einer „Nationalpolitischen Bildungsanstalt" (NAPOLA) des NS-Regimes umgewidmet. Nach dem Zweiten Weltkrieg war im Schloss ein staatliches Internat untergebracht. Seit 2002 ist es Sitz einer gemeinnützigen Stiftung.

Duke Johann Ernst of Schleswig-Holstein-Sonderburg-Plön constructed the palace of Plön as a mighty renaissance palace from 1633 to 1636. The palace is a three winged brick building, with the court of honor opening out onto the Greater Lake of Plön. The gardens by Georg Dietrich Tschierske have been planned in baroque style. They were formed to a landscape garden in the 19th century. In 1761 the palace fell into the hands of the Danish royal family and after 1867 to the province of Schleswig-Holstein. From the imperial era until 1920 the palace of Plön was a Prussian cadet school. In the Weimar Republic it was a state-run educational establishment. Since 1933 it served as an elite national political academy of the fascist regime. After the Second World War the palace of Plön has hosted a federally run boarding school. Since 2002 the palace has belonged to a non-profit endowment.

Gut Salzau

Fargau-Pratjau, Kreis Plön

Salzau, am Selenter See gelegen, fand als Rittersitz erstmals im späteren 13. Jahrhundert Erwähnung. Benannt nach dem Ritter Otto von Salzau, wurde das Herrenhaus im 18. Jahrhundert in barocken Formen umgebaut. Nach einem verheerenden Brand veranlasste Otto Graf Blome, dessen Familie Gut Salzau bis ins 20. Jahrhundert hinein besaß, 1882 den kompletten Wiederaufbau im neoklassizistischen Stil. Eingebettet in die grüne Holsteiner Landschaft ist die Anlage eines der größten Herrenhäuser des späten 19. Jahrhunderts. Das prunkvolle Gebäude umgibt ein wunderschöner Park. Seit fast zwanzig Jahren befindet sich Salzau samt einigen Nebengebäuden im Besitz des Landes Schleswig-Holstein. Inzwischen hat das Landeskulturzentrum seinen Sitz in Gut Salzau gefunden. Dem „Schleswig-Holstein-Musik-Festival" dient es im Sommer als Veranstaltungsort.

Salzau on Selenter Lake was first mentioned in the 13th century as a knightly post. Named after Knight Otto von Salzau, the hall was reconstructed in the 18th century in baroque forms. After a devastating fire, the palace was completely reconstructed in neo-classical style by Otto Graf Blome, in whose family the palace remained until the 20th century. Imbedded in the green landscape of Holstein, the palace of Salzau is one of the largest halls of the late 19th century. The pompous building is surrounded by a lovely park. Since nearly 20 years the palace, together with its surrounding buildings, is the property of the state of Schleswig-Holstein. It houses the region's cultural center and serves as a location of the Schleswig-Holstein Music Festival each summer.

Schloss Eutin

Eutin, Schleswig-Holstein

Das Eutiner Schloss ging 1156 aus dem Haus des Bischofs Gerold hervor und wurde im späten 13. Jahrhundert zur Burg ausgebaut. Die aus Backstein errichtete vierflügelige Anlage umschließt einen Hof mit hell verputzten Wänden, die Schauseite ist zur Stadt gerichtet. Ein Wassergraben umgibt den Bau, der sein heutiges Aussehen durch den schwedischen Hofbaumeister Rudolph Matthias Dallin in den Jahren 1717 bis 1727 erhielt. Im Schlosspark lernte die spätere Zarin Katharina die Große den Prinzen Karl Peter Ulrich von Holstein-Gottorf kennen, der 1762 zum russischen Zaren Peter III. gekrönt wurde. Der Park wurde Ende des 18. Jahrhunderts in einen Landschaftsgarten im englischen Stil umgewandelt. Die Großherzöge von Oldenburg wählten Eutin 1803 zu ihrer Nebenresidenz. 1992 brachte die herzogliche Familie Schloss und Garten in eine Stiftung ein. Heute ist das Eutiner Schloss größtenteils als Museum öffentlich zugänglich.

The palace of Eutin has its origins in the house of Bishop Gerold in 1156, which was expanded into a castle in the late 13th century. The brick four-wing layout encloses a courtyard with brightly plastered walls with the obverse of the palace directed toward the city. A moat surrounds the building that was constructed from 1717 until 1727 by the architect of the Swedish Court, Rudolph Matthias Dallin. Tsarina Katherine the Great met Prince Karl Peter Ulrich von Holstein-Gottorf (who was crowned Russian Tsar Peter III in 1762) first in the palace gardens. The park was converted into a scenic landscape garden in the English style at the close of the 18th century. The Grand-Dukes of Oldenburg chose Eutin to be their second residence in 1803. In 1992 the noble family placed the family palace and gardens into an endowment. Today the majority of the palace of Eutin is accessible to the public as a museum.

Schloss Tremsbüttel

Tremsbüttel, Kreis Stormarn

Als dänischer Amtssitz des Grafen zu Stolberg 1777 erwähnt, ging das Herrenhaus Tremsbüttel 1895 an den Remscheider Unternehmer Fritz Hasenclever, der das Schloss vom Berliner Architekten Hans Grisebach im Stil der Neo-Renaissance umgestalten ließ – diese Spielart des Historismus war eine Vorliebe des eher deutsch-national gesinnten Großbürgertums. Bis zur Mitte des 20. Jahrhunderts als großbürgerliches Gut in Betrieb, wechselte Tremsbüttel 1949 erneut den Besitzer. Konsul Siegfried Zimmermann machte aus dem Gutsbetrieb ein erfolgreiches Schlosshotel. Berühmte Zeitgenossen wie die Beatles, die Rolling Stones, Klaus Kinski, Heinz Rühmann, Sophia Loren oder Leonard Bernstein brachten den Jet-Set nach Tremsbüttel. 1996 erwarb die Unternehmerfamilie Strathmann den Betrieb. Das Gebäude wurde restauriert und zu einem Kommunikationszentrum für Empfänge und Tagungen erweitert.

The palace of Tremsbüttel was named the Danish official residence of Count Stolberg in 1777. In 1895 the palace went to the entrepreneur Fritz Hasenclever of Remscheid, who entrusted architect Hans Grisebach of Berlin to remodel the palace in neo-renaissance style. This historicism was a particular preference of the patriotic and nationally-minded upper class. Until the mid-20th century it served as an upper-class manor, though it changed ownership in 1949. Consul Siegfried Zimmermann made the estate into a successful palace hotel. Famous contemporaries such as the Beatles, the Rolling Stones, the German actors Klaus Kinski and Heinz Rühmann, Sophia Loren and Leonard Bernstein brought jet-set live to Tremsbüttel. In 1969 the entrepreneurial Strathmann family bought the palace hotel. The building was restored and expanded into a center for communication, which hosts receptions and conferences.

Schloss Ahrensburg

Ahrensburg, Kreis Stormarn

Auf einer von einem Wassergraben umgebenen Insel liegt das weiße Renaissance-Schloss Ahrensburg, das Ende der 1570er Jahre für Peter Rantzau erbaut wurde. Das dreischiffige Schloss wird von vier schlanken, achteckigen Türmen flankiert. Die nebeneinander liegenden Langhäuser sind charakteristisch für die holsteinische Gutsarchitektur. Die Rantzauer residierten hier fast sieben Generationen lang, bis das Gut 1759 von Heinrich Carl von Schimmelmann erworben und innen im Stil des Rokoko umgestaltet wurde. Schloss Ahrensburg ist einer der schönsten Renaissancebauten Schleswig-Holsteins und gehört seit 1955 als „Museum der schleswig-holsteinischen Adelskultur" zu den Hauptsehenswürdigkeiten des Landes. Anfang 2003 in eine private Stiftung umgewandelt, stehen Schloss, Schlossinsel und Park unter Denkmalschutz.

The white renaissance palace of Ahrensburg lies on a moat-surrounded island. It was built at the end of the 1570s for Peter Rantzau. The tri-naved palace is flanked by four narrow octagonal towers. The parallel lying naves are characteristic of manor architecture of the Holstein region. The Rantzau family lived here nearly seven generations, until the manor was purchased by Heinrich Carl von Schimmelmann in 1759 and redecorated inside in the rococo style. The palace of Ahrensburg is one of the most beautiful renaissance buildings of Schleswig-Holstein and in 1955 became 'Museum of the Aristocratic Culture of Schleswig-Holstein'. It is one of the main tourist sights of the region. In 2003 it became a private endowment and the palace, island, and palace gardens are under historic landmark protection.

Schloss Celle

Celle, Niedersachsen

Seit 1378 residierten die Herzöge von Braunschweig-Lüneburg in Celle, ließen eine ältere Burganlage zum Schloss erweitern und später in mehreren Bauphasen verändern. Inspiriert von einem Aufenthalt in Italien, erteilte Herzog Georg Wilhelm 1670 den Auftrag, den damaligen Renaissancebau zu modernisieren, die Fassade im venezianischen Stil zu gestalten und ein barockes Hoftheater zu erbauen, das von wechselnden Ensembles bespielt wurde. Auffallend sind das von Giebeln umrahmte Dach und die markanten Ecktürme. Das auf einer Insel liegende und von einem Wassergraben umgebene Celler Schloss war seit 1772 Verbannungsort der dänischen Königin Caroline Mathilde, deren Affäre mit dem Arzt Johann Friedrich Struensee mit dessen Hinrichtung geendet hatte. Ihr Schicksal literarisierte Per Olov Enquist in dem Buch „Der Besuch des Leibarztes".

Since 1378 the dukes of Braunschweig-Lüneburg lived in Celle. They upgraded an old castle into a palace and over the years adapted it through various building phases. In 1670 Duke Georg Wilhelm, inspired by his time in Italy, gave the order to modernize the then renaissance building. He had the facades reconstructed into Venetian style and built a baroque court theater, where changing ensembles performed. Remarkable are the gable-framed roof and prominent corner towers. The Palace of Celle, which lies on an island and is surrounded by a moat, was off-limits from 1772 to Queen Caroline Mathilde of Denmark, whose affair with Doctor Johann Friedrich Struensee ended with his execution. Their fate was novelized by Per Olov Enquist in the book 'The Royal Physician's Visit'.

Schloss Gifhorn

Gifhorn, Niedersachsen

Das trapezförmig um einen Innenhof angelegte Schloss im Stil der Weserrenaissance entstand von 1525 bis 1581. Auftraggeber waren Herzog Ernst der Bekenner von Braunschweig-Lüneburg und sein in Celle residierender Bruder Otto. Schloss Gifhorn lag im Zentrum einer Wehranlage, die der Festungsbaumeister Michael Clare aus Celle plante. Er ließ rundherum Wälle aufschütten und hohe Mauern mit Bastionstürmen an den Ecken errichten, von denen unterirdische Verbindungsgänge ins Schloss führten. Der breite Wassergraben ließ sich nur über eine schmale Brücke passieren. Zudem konnte die Umgebung geflutet und in einen unwegsamen Sumpf verwandelt werden. Die Festung wurde seit 1770 zurückgebaut. Am Dach des Torhauses – des ältesten Gebäudeteils – befinden sich auffällige, in dieser Form nur hier erhaltene Halbkreisgiebel.

This trapezoid-shaped palace in the style of the Weser-Renaissance with its internal courtyard was constructed between 1525 and 1581. The benefactors were Duke Ernst the Confessor of Braunschweig-Lüneburg and his brother Otto who resided in Celle. The palace of Gifhorn was situated in the center of a fortified area, planned by the fortress builder, Michael Clare of Celle. He had it encircled by ramparts and high walls with battalion towers on the corners, from which underground tunnels connected into the palace. The wide moat could be crossed only by a thin bridge. The area could also be flooded and transformed into an impassible swamp. The fortress was partly demolished in 1770. The roof of the gatehouse, the oldest portion of the structure, contains striking semi-circular gables, which survived in this form only here.

Schloss Wolfsburg

Wolfsburg, Niedersachsen

Ein „Wolfsburg" genannter, von Wassergräben umgebener Wohnturm („Motte") war schon zu Beginn des 14. Jahrhunderts im Besitz des Geschlechts von Bartensleben, das den Wolf zu seinem Wappentier gewählt hatte. Der vierflügelige, um einen Innenhof gelegene repräsentative Bau von Schloss Wolfsburg wurde um 1620 im Stil der Weserrenaissance vollendet. Als Baumeister ist Johann Edeler aus Hameln überliefert. 1747 fiel das Schloss per Erbfolge an die Familie von der Schulenburg. Diese ließ einen barocken Lustgarten anlegen, später kam ein Landschaftspark hinzu. 1942 wurde die Familie von der Schulenburg enteignet, um auf großen Teilen ihrer Ländereien das Volkswagen-Werk zu erweitern. Schloss Wolfsburg wird heute für kulturelle Einrichtungen und repräsentative Veranstaltungen genutzt.

A residential tower surrounded by a moat ('motte') which was called 'Wolfsburg' (wolf's castle) was already owned by the von Bartensleben family, which selected the wolf as its heraldic animal, at the beginning of the 14th century. The four-storey representative 'Wolfsburg' centered around a courtyard was completed in 1620 in the Weser-Renaissance style. The supervisor of construction is listed as Johann Edeler from Hameln. The house fell into the hands of the von der Schulenburg family through inheritance in 1747. They added a baroque pleasure garden and later a scenic landscape garden. In 1942 the von der Schulenburg family was dispossessed of the estate in order to extend the Volkswagen works. The palace of Wolfsburg is now used as a cultural facility and for representative events.

Schloss Schwerin

Schwerin, Mecklenburg

Die strategisch günstige Situation einer flachen Insel am Ufer des Schweriner Sees nutzten bereits Menschen der jüngeren Steinzeit. Im 9./10. Jahrhundert existierte hier eine obotritische Burg, die gegen 1167 Sitz der Schweriner Grafen wurde. 1358 erwarben die Herzöge von Mecklenburg den Grafentitel und siedelten auf die Schweriner Inselburg um. Hier residierten sie fast ohne Unterbrechung bis 1918. Der heutige, sehr einheitlich wirkende Baubestand geht auf mit ihren Terrakottagiebeln charakteristische Bauteile des 16. Jahrhunderts zurück, die der niederländische Baumeister Ghert Evert Piloot im 17. Jahrhundert erweiterte. Im 19. Jahrhundert wurde Hofbaumeister Georg Adolph Demmler mit einem tiefgreifenden Umbau beauftragt, für den er die Renaissanceteile des Schlosses selbst und das französische Loire-Schloss Chambord zum Vorbild nahm: In Erinnerung an das ideale Staatskloster „Thelema" in Rabelais' Schelmenroman „Gargantua und Pantagruel" schuf Demmler eine typisch historistische Allegorie des Sitzes eines gerechten und weisen Herrschers. Heute residiert hier der Landtag Mecklenburg-Vorpommerns.

The strategic situation of a level island on the banks of the Schweriner See presented an ideal situation for human civilization already in the early Stone Age. An Obotrite castle stood there in the 9th and 10th centuries, which became the residence of the Count of Schwerin around 1167. In 1358, the Dukes of Mecklenburg inherited the titles of Count and resettled on the Island-castle of Schwerin. They lived here nearly uninterrupted until 1918. Today, the extremely unified looking collection as built can be traced back to parts of the building characteristic of the 16th century, such as the terracotta gables. Additions were made by the Dutch architect, Ghert Evert Piloot, in the 17th century. In the 19th century the architect of the Court, Georg Adolph Demmler, was assigned a dramatic renovation for which he used the renaissance portions of the palace and the French Loire-chateau Chambord as an inspiration. In honor of the idealizing state cloister 'Thelema' in Rabelais' picturesque novel, 'Gargantua and Pantagruel', Demmler created a typical historical allegory of the seat of a just and wise ruler. Today the exemplarily restored building houses the Parliament of Mecklenburg-Vorpommern.

Schloss Ludwigslust

Ludwigslust, Mecklenburg

Die mecklenburgische Residenz Ludwigslust entstand ab 1763/64 nach Plänen des Hofbaumeisters Johann Joachim Busch. Herzog Friedrich der Fromme ließ sie an Stelle eines älteren Jagdschlosses als mecklenburgische Hauptresidenz errichten. Als erstes legte Busch einen 28 Kilometer langen Kanal mit Wasserkünsten an, der prägendes Element des Schlossparks wurde. Anschließend plante der Hofbaumeister das frühklassizistische Schloss, die Schlosskirche, die mit pittoresken Architekturen ausgeschmückten Gartenanlagen, Plätze und eine Stadtanlage. Alle Teile sind durch axiale Beziehungen zu einem einzigartigen Ensemble miteinander verbunden, das Peter Joseph Lenné Mitte des 19. Jahrhunderts durch einen Landschaftsgarten erweiterte – als der mecklenburgische Hof bereits wieder in Schwerin residierte und Ludwigslust nur noch Sommerresidenz war. Das Schloss, dessen Ausstattung weitgehend erhalten ist, wird museal genutzt.

The residence of Ludwigslust in Mecklenburg was erected in 1763 and 1764 according to the plans of court architect, Johann Joachim Busch. Duke Friedrich der Fromme (Friedrich the Pious) had it built as the cardinal residence of Mecklenburg in the former location of an old hunting palace. Busch initially constructed a 28 kilometer-long canal with water games to be the signature element of the palace gardens. Finally, the court architect planned an early-Classicist palace, palace church, gardens with their picturesque architecture, circuses, and a town-grid. All parts of the estate are joined into an ensemble through a series of axial relationships, which Peter Joseph Lenné furthered through a scenic garden in the middle of the 19th century when the court of Mecklenburg again resided in Schwerin, and Ludwigslust was only used as a summer residence. The furnishings of the palace have remained extensively intact. Ludwigslust is used as a museum.

Schloss Boitzenburg

Boitzenburg, Uckermark / Brandenburg

Im Mittelalter gab es auf der Insel in der Uckermark, auf der Schloss Boitzenburg liegt, eine 1276 erstmals erwähnte Burg („castrum Bonceneborch"). Seit 1528 war hier das Stammschloss der Familie von Arnim, das sich verändernden Bedürfnissen durch An- und Umbauten kontinuierlich angepasst wurde. Im 18. Jahrhundert entschied man sich schließlich für eine repräsentative Gestaltung des Anwesens und verlagerte alle Wirtschaftsgebäude als Gutshof auf ein Territorium außerhalb der Insel. Damit bot sich Raum zu deren Anlage als englischer Landschaftspark. Der Baumeister Friedrich August Stüler erhielt 1838 den Auftrag, einen Teil des Schlosses um ein Stockwerk zu erhöhen und im Tudorstil zu verändern. Zeitgleich plante der Landschaftsarchitekt Peter Joseph Lenné die Erweiterung des Schlossparks. Schon wenige Jahrzehnte später, 1881 bis 1884, wurden einzelne Bauteile im Stil der Neo-Renaissance umgebaut, um dem Ensemble insgesamt ein geschlossenes Aussehen zu geben.

The castle first mentioned in 1276 as 'castrum Bonceneborch', became known later as Boitzenburg. It stands on an island in the region of the Uckermark (northern Brandenburg). Since 1528 it was the palace of the von Arnim family which continually adapted the palace through renovations and additions. In the 18th century a decision was made to have a more prestigious arrangement of the estate, and all agricultural buildings were displaced to a manor in a territory off of the island. This offered space on the grounds for the construction of an English landscape park. The Berlin architect, Friedrich August Stüler received an appointment in 1838 to add an additional storey to part of the palace and to redesign it in the Tudor style. Simultaneously landscape architect, Peter Joseph Lenné planned the extension of the palace gardens. Already a few decades later, from 1881 to 1884, portions of the residence were rebuilt in the style of the Neo-Renaissance in order to give the entire ensemble a cohesive appearance.

Schloss Rheinsberg

Rheinsberg, Brandenburg

Am Ufer des nördlich Berlins gelegenen Grienericksees gab es im Mittelalter eine Wasserburg. In der Renaissance errichtete man an gleicher Stelle ein Schloss, das Friedrich Wilhelm I. seinem Sohn Kronprinz Friedrich, später Friedrich II., schenkte. Dieser ließ das schön gelegene Schloss Rheinsberg bis 1740 von Johann G. Kemmeter und Georg W. von Knobelsdorff im später sogenannten Stil des Friderizianischen Rokoko umbauen. Er verbrachte dort nach eigenen Worten die glücklichste Zeit seines Lebens. Seit 1752 lebte Friedrichs vielseitig gebildeter Bruder Prinz Heinrich mit seiner Ehefrau Wilhelmine von Hessen-Kassel in Schloss Rheinsberg, etablierte dort einen Musenhof und ließ sich schließlich 1802 im Park in einer Grabpyramide beisetzen.

In the Middle Ages there was a moated castle on the bank of Grienerick Lake, which lies to the north of Berlin. During the renaissance a new palace was erected in the same place, which King Friedrich Wilhelm I gave to his son, Crown-prince Friedrich (later Friedrich II the Great). Friedrich II had the beautifully situated Palace Rheinsberg renovated in the later-termed 'Friderizianisches Rokoko' until 1740 by Johann G. Kemmeter and Georg W. von Knobelsdorff. According to his own words, he spent the happiest period of his life there. Beginning in 1752, Friedrich's multi-faceted brother Prince Heinrich and his wife, Wilhelmine von Hessen-Kassel lived in Rheinsberg Palace where they established a courtyard for artists and poets. Heinrich was finally laid to rest in a pyramid in the palace gardens in 1802.

Schloss Liebenberg

Liebenberg, Brandenburg

Das 1745 erbaute Barockschloss mit separatem Gutshof und dem „Seehaus" am Große-Lankesee ist von einem bemerkenswerten Landschaftspark nach englischem Vorbild umgeben, den der preußische Gartenarchitekt Peter Joseph Lenné entworfen hat. Im Park liegt das Lindenhaus, und ein von alten Bäumen umstandenes barockes Teehaus lädt zum Verweilen ein. Der damalige Besitzer Philipp zu Eulenburg (1847–1921) lud Kaiser Wilhelm II. mehrmals zur „Kaiserjagd" in den Wäldern rund um Schloss Liebenberg ein. Im „Seehaus" traf sich während des Zweiten Weltkriegs die Widerstandsgruppe „Rote Kapelle" um das Ehepaar Schulze-Boysen.

The baroque palace with a separate farm building and a lake house on the Greater Lanke Lake is surrounded by one of the most remarkable scenic landscape parks that the Prussian landscape architect Peter Joseph Lenné ever designed. The park includes the 'Lindenhaus' ('lime tree house'), and a baroque tea house surrounded by aged trees, both which invite the visitor to linger. The former occupant, Philipp zu Eulenburg (1847–1921), invited Emperor Wilhelm II more than once to an 'Emperor's Hunt' in the forest around Palace Liebenberg. The lake house was the meeting point of the 'Rote Kapelle' ('Red Chapel'), a resistance group of World War II around the Schulze-Boysen couple.

45

Schloss Oranienburg

Oranienburg, Mark Brandenburg

Beeinflusst von niederländischen Vorbildern erbauten Johann Gregor Memhardt und Michael Matthias Smids seit 1651 einen Landsitz für den Großen Kurfürsten Friedrich und seine Frau Louise Henriette von Oranien-Nassau, der zu ihren Ehren den Namen Oranienburg erhielt. Von 1689 bis 1709 wurde das Renaissanceschloss im Auftrag ihres Sohnes Kurfürst Friedrich III. von Johann Arnold Nering und Johann Friedrich Eosander zu einem barocken Corps de Logis mit zwei Seitenflügeln umgebaut und mit Tapisserien, Skulpturen und Gemälden prächtig ausgestattet. In Deckengemälden wird die Bedeutung des Hauses Oranien-Nassau allegorisiert. August Wilhelm von Preußen ließ Oranienburg Mitte des 18. Jahrhunderts im Stil des später sogenannten Friderizianischen Rokoko modernisieren.

Influenced by Dutch examples, Johann Gregor Memhardt and Michael Matthias Smids began to build a country residence in 1651 for the Great Elector Friedrich and his wife Louise Henriette von Oranien-Nassau. In her honor, it received the name Oranienburg. From 1689 to 1709 the renaissance palace was by the order of their son, Elector Friedrich III, to be remodeled into a baroque Corps de Logis with two side wings. Tapestries, sculptures, and paintings were to be added to magnificently furnish it. Ceiling murals allegorize the significance of the House of Oranien-Nassau. August Wilhelm of Prussia modernized Oranienburg in the style of the later-named 'Friderizianisches Rokoko' (rococo from the period of Friedrich the Great) in the middle of the 18th century.

Schloss Charlottenburg

Berlin-Charlottenburg

Der seit 1695 im Auftrag der Kurfürstin Sophie Charlotte, Ehefrau Friedrichs III., von Johann A. Nehring erbaute barocke Corps de Logis war ursprünglich eine außerhalb Berlins auf dem Lande gelegene Sommerresidenz. Namhafte Architekten wie Eosander, Schlüter, Langhans und von Knobelsdorff erweiterten das Lustschloss mit Anbauten und ergänzten es durch im Park gelegene separate Gebäude – Schlosstheater, Orangerie, „Schinkelpavillon", Grabmal für Königin Luise. Heute ist der als Museum genutzte langgestreckte Kuppelbau eines der architektonischen Wahrzeichen Berlins. Der Barockgarten weitet sich zum Landschaftspark mit altem Baumbestand, ist Teil der Großstadt geworden und bei den Bewohnern des inzwischen eng bebauten Innenstadtbezirks als Naherholungsgebiet beliebt.

Built by the order of Electoral Princess Sophie Charlotte, wife of Friedrich III in 1695 by Johann A. Nehring, the baroque Corps de Logis was originally intended to be a summer residence in the countryside outside of Berlin. Well-known architects such as Eosander, Schlüter, Langhans and von Knobelsdorff expanded the pleasure palace with additions and completed it with separate lying buildings in the garden: the palace theater, orangery, the famous 'Schinkel-pavilion', and a mausoleum for Queen Louise. Today used as a museum, the long, domed building is one of the architectural emblems of Berlin. The baroque garden expands into a scenic landscape park with an old tree population which has become surrounded by the city. It is popular as a recreational area by residents who live among the closely cropped buildings of the city center.

Schloss Bellevue

Berlin-Tiergarten

Der nahe dem Tiergarten gelegene Amtssitz des deutschen Bundespräsidenten entstand bis 1786 als Lustschloss für Ferdinand von Preußen, den jüngeren Bruder Friedrichs II. Der Architekt Michael Philipp Boumann integrierte Teile eines Vorgängerbaus in eine frühklassizistische Dreiflügelanlage mit zweieinhalb Geschossen. 1844 richtete Friedrich Wilhelm IV. hier die „Vaterländische Galerie" ein, das erste Museum für zeitgenössische Kunst in Preußen. 1938 baute der Architekt Paul Baumgarten das damals ungenutzte Schloss zum Gästehaus der Reichsregierung um. In den 1950er Jahren erhielt es, in seiner neuen Funktion als Zweitsitz des Bundespräsidenten, eine – in zwei Räumen erhaltene – Inneneinrichtung im Stile der Zeit. Die Restaurierung von 1986/87 versetzte den Bau äußerlich in den Ursprungszustand. Auch nach dem Umzug der Bundesregierung von Bonn nach Berlin nutzen die Bundespräsidenten Bellevue für repräsentative Anlässe. 1996 bis 1998 entstand unmittelbar benachbart das markante Bundespräsidialamt nach Plänen von Martin Gruber und Helmut Kleine-Kraneburg.

The pleasure palace for Ferdinand of Prussia, the younger brother of Friedrich II, was built in 1786 near Tiergarten and is now the official residence of the German Federal President. Architect Michael Philipp Boumann integrated parts of a former building in an early classicist three-wing construction with two and a half floors. In 1844 Friedrich Wilhelm IV organized the first museum of contemporary art in Prussia, called the 'Gallery of the Fatherland' here. In 1938 architect Paul Baumgarten renovated the then unused palace into a guest house for the government of the 'Reich'. In the 1950s it received the new function of the second home of the Federal President. Two rooms conserve the interior decoration in the style of the time. The restoration of the building in 1986 and 1987 transferred the exterior of the building back to its original condition. After the relocation of the federal government from Bonn to Berlin, Palace Bellevue has been used by the Federal President for official occasions. According to the plans of Martin Gruber and Helmut Kleine-Kraneburg the striking administration building for the Presidency was erected immediately adjacent to Palace Bellevue from 1996 to 1998.

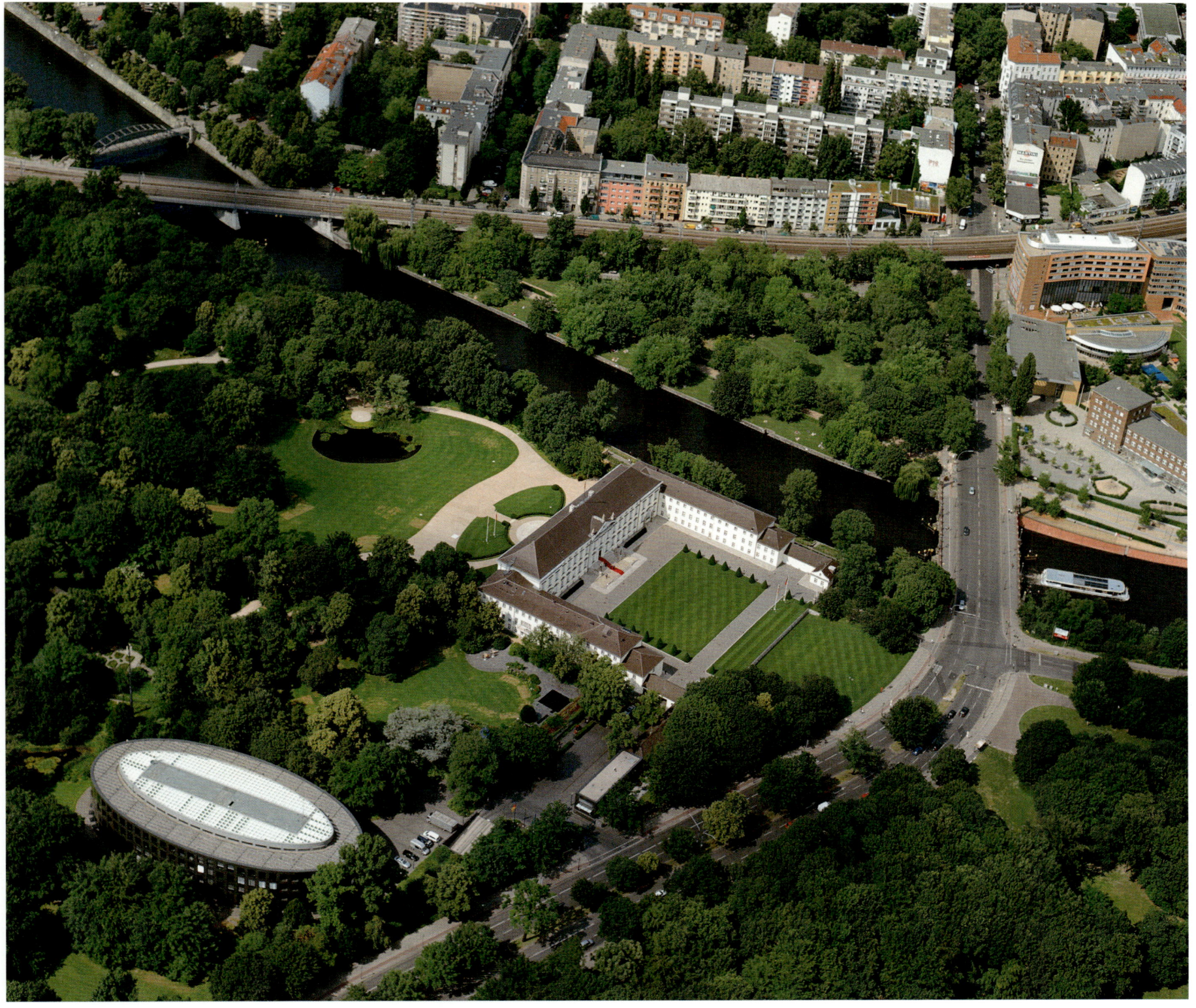

Schloss Sanssouci

Potsdam, Brandenburg

Leicht gebaute Rokokoarchitektur für den Sommer, die oberhalb einer sechsstufigen Terrassenanlage mit Weinstöcken und Feigenbäumen am Bornstedter Höhenzug prangt: Das ist Schloss Sanssouci („ohne Sorge"). Friedrich II. (der Große) hatte Ideenskizzen für sein 1745 bis 1747 erbautes stilvolles „Lust-Haus zu Potsdam" angefertigt. Die Umsetzung der Entwurfszeichnungen zu einem eingeschossigen Corps de Logis – den in der Mitte eine Kuppel bekrönt – mit kurzen, bergseitig gelegenen Pavillons und Kolonnadenhof übernahm der Architekt Georg Wenzeslaus von Knobelsdorff. Er ließ auch den barocken Lustgarten mit ausladendem Wasserbecken im Parterre unterhalb Sanssoucis anlegen. Zudem entstand eine Orangerie und wenig später die berühmte Bildergalerie. In der Ära Friedrich Wilhelms IV., 1840 bis 1842, verlängerte man – nach Plänen von Ludwig Persius – die Pavillons zu Seitenflügeln parallel zur Schlossachse.

Built to be airy for the summer, this piece of rococo architecture stands on the top of a six-storied terrace construction with grape-vines and fig trees on the Bornsted Mountain Range: it is Palace Sanssouci ('without worries'). Friedrich the Great himself draw the initial sketches for his stylish 'pleasure house in Potsdam' which was built from 1745 to 1747. The transformation of the preliminary drawings to a single-storey Corps de Logis, crowned in the center by a dome, with short upward-facing pavilions and a colonnade courtyard were overseen by architect Georg Wenzeslaus von Knobelsdorff. The baroque pleasure garden with an extended water basin constructed in the garden parterre beneath Sanssouci follows his plans, too. In addition an orangery and a bit later the famous picture gallery were built. In the era of Friedrich Wilhelm IV from plans by Ludwig Persius, the side wing pavilions were lengthened parallel to the axis of the palace from 1840 to 1842.

Schloss Babelsberg

Potsdam-Babelsberg

Inmitten der Flusslandschaft der Havel wurde Schloss Babelsberg 1834 bis 1849 als Sommerresidenz für das spätere Kaiserpaar Wilhelm I. und Augusta erbaut. Karl Friedrich Schinkel und sein Schüler Ludwig Persius ließen sich bei der Gestaltung des neogotischen Backsteinbaus mit seinen prägnanten Rundtürmen und großen Spitzbogenfenstern vom englischen Tudorstil inspirieren. Ihr Nachfolger Johann Heinrich Strack erweiterte das Gebäude auf Wunsch der Auftraggeber durch Anbauten, veränderte die Fassadengliederung mit Erkern, Söllern und unterschiedlichen Fenstern („Burgenstil"). Englische Landschaftsgärten wirkten bei der Anlage des großzügig bemessenen Parks stilbildend. Dessen Planung mit reizvollen Sichtachsen hinüber nach Glienicke und freiem Blick auf die Stadtsilhouette Potsdams übernahmen Peter Joseph Lenné und Fürst Pückler-Muskau – zwei Großmeister der Gartenarchitektur.

Palace Babelsberg was built between 1834 and 1849 in the striking landscape of the River Havel as the summer residence for the couple Wilhelm I und Augusta (who later became emperor and empress). Karl Friedrich Schinkel and his successor, Ludwig Persius created the shape of the neo-gothic brick building with its pithy round towers and large lancet windows, which was inspired by the English Tudor-style. Their successor, Johann Heinrich Strack expanded the building at the wish of his client through different portions, and changed the appearance of the façade with oriels, galleries, and different windows in the 'Burgenstil' (castle style). English landscape gardens were models for the layout of the generously sized garden. Two masters of landscape architecture, Peter Joseph Lenné and Fürst Pückler-Muskau, oversaw the planning of the gardens and their charming 'Sichtachsen' (viewing axes) toward Glienicke and the open view of the skyline of Potsdam.

Schloss Neuhardenberg

Neuhardenberg, Oderbruch/Brandenburg

Zwischen 1786 und 1789 wurde im Oderbruch das damals sogenannte Schloss Quilitz als eingeschossiges Gebäude mit Mansarddach erbaut. Dieses Anwesen erhielt der preußische Staatskanzler und Reformator Karl August Freiherr von Hardenberg zum Dank für seine Verdienste 1814 zum Geschenk und benannte es bald darauf in Neu-Hardenberg um. Fünf Jahre später beauftragte Hardenberg den Architekten Karl Friedrich Schinkel damit, den Bau zu modernisieren und zu vergrößern. Dieser konzipierte das heute als Hotel und Tagungsort, für Konzerte, Theateraufführungen und Ausstellungen genutzte elegante zweigeschossige klassizistische Palais. Der Gartenarchitekt Peter Joseph Lenné war federführend bei der Gestaltung des Landschaftsparks – so hat sich in Neuhardenberg bis heute eine stimmige Synthese von Natur und Architektur ergeben.

Then called Quilitz Palace, Neuhardenberg Palace was built between 1786 und 1789 as a single-storey building with a mansard roof. It was this estate which Prussian Chancellor and reformer Karl August Freiherr von Hardenberg received in thanks for his years of public service. Shortly after, it was renamed 'Neu-Hardenberg' ('New-Hardenberg'). Five years later Hardenberg hired architect, Karl Friedrich Schinkel, to modernize and enlarge the building. The Prussian landscape architect, Peter Joseph Lenné, was in charge of the layout of the scenic park, so even today Neuhardenberg produces a harmonious synthesis of nature and architecture. In today's form, the elegant two-storey classicist palace is used as a hotel and meeting place, for concerts, performances, and exhibitions.

Schloss Branitz

Branitz bei Cottbus, Brandenburg

Inmitten eines „Pleasuregrounds" mit Blumenrabatten und Ziergehölzen gelegen, ist Schloss Branitz das architektonische Zentrum des von Hermann Fürst Pückler-Muskau (1785–1871) im englischen Stil konzipierten Landschaftsparks. Pücklers Gartendenkmal wird von Wasserläufen, Teichen, zu Ensembles gruppierten oder als Solitäre wirkenden Bäumen und architektonischen Kabinettstücken geprägt, zwischen denen der Blick auf weiträumigen Sichtachsen den Park durchmisst. Einzigartig in diesem Gartenensemble sind die Seepyramide, in der sich der reiselustige Fürst bestatten ließ, und eine als Aussichtspunkt gestaltete Landpyramide. Das historisch möblierte Schloss aus dem späten Barock (1770–1772) umgeben typische Ensemblebauten wie Marstall und Kavaliershaus. Bei einem Rundgang bestechen vor allem die prächtigen „orientalischen" Zimmer.

Branitz Palace in the middle of pleasure grounds with flowerbeds and flowering trees is the architectural center of an English-style landscape park conceived by Hermann Fürst Pückler-Muskau (1785–1871). Pückler's garden monument is enhanced with running streams, ponds, and solitary and grouped ensembles of trees and architectural showpieces, which give point de vues to far-reaching viewing axes. Unique to the garden ensemble is a land pyramid, which serves as a vantage point, and the spectacular lake pyramid in which the Prince had himself entombed. The historically furnished palace from the late baroque period (1770–1772) is surrounded by typical ensemble constructions such as stables and a cavalier house. Above all, the pompous 'oriential' rooms, is especially captivating in tours of the palace.

Albrechtsburg

Meißen, Sachsen

Die Anlage hoch über dem Elbtal gilt als bedeutendste spätmittelalterliche Burg Deutschlands. Der sächsische Kurfürst Ernst und Herzog Albrecht von Meißen übertrugen gemeinsam dem „obersten Werkmeister" des Hauses Wettin, Arnold von Sachsen, 1470 den Neubau nördlich des Meißener Doms. Nach der Aufteilung des sächsischen Territoriums 1485 verlief der Weiterbau schleppend, erst 1521 ließ Herzog Georg der Bärtige den Bau von Jakob Heilmann vollenden. Das Bauwerk auf hakenförmigem Grundriss hat mehrere Türme, die von einer riesigen Dachfläche mit Lukarnen zusammengebunden werden. So ergibt sich für den Gesamtbau selbst eine turmartige Gestalt, was als Symbol der politischen und wirtschaftlichen Macht der Wettiner gedeutet wird. Das der verfeinerten Hofkultur seiner Zeit entsprechende Raumprogramm besticht durch eine ausgeklügelte Funktionalität. Viele Räume haben aufwendige spätgotische Gewölbe. Sehenswert ist der Große Treppenturm, ein Meisterwerk damaliger Steinmetzkunst. Die Albrechtsburg war von 1710 bis 1863 Sitz der berühmten sächsischen Porzellanmanufaktur. Heute ist sie Museum.

The solitary estate situated high above the Elbe River Valley is considered one of the most distinguished late-medieval castles of Germany. In 1470 Elector Ernst of Saxony and Duke Albrecht of Meißen commissioned the 'most distinguished foreman' of the House of Wettin, Arnold von Sachsen, to build the new structure north of the Cathedral of Meißen. After the division of the territories of Saxony in 1485, the progress on the construction became sluggish. It wasn't until 1521 that Duke Georg the Bearded had Jakob Heilmann complete the building. The construction has a hook-shaped layout and many towers that are bound together by an enormous roof with lucarnes. This tower-like over all construction was meant to be interpreted as a symbol of the political and economic power of the Wettin family. The refined courtly culture of the time period captivates with a well thought out functionality in room planning. Many rooms can be seen with late gothic vaulted-ceilings. The grand stair tower is a masterwork of stone masonry of the time period. Albrechtsburg was the site of the famous Saxon porcelain factory from 1710 until 1863, now it is a museum.

Schloss Moritzburg

Moritzburg bei Dresden

Ein Vorgängerbau des 16. Jahrhunderts mit vier durch Mauern miteinander verbundenen Rundtürmen hat die Figur des heutigen Schlosses Moritzburg vorgeprägt. August der Starke plante ab 1703 einen Umbau dieser Anlage zu einem inmitten eines Sees gelegenen Bauwerk, zu dem er ab 1716 Matthäus Daniel Pöppelmann heranzog. Pöppelmann orientierte die bestehende Anlage um und bildete ihren Grundriss um zwei Ehrenhöfe H-förmig aus. Der Baumeister erhöhte zwei Türme um zwei Geschosse, errichtete die beiden anderen neu und bekrönte sie mit den charakteristischen welschen Hauben und Laternen. Der Zentralbau wurde nach den Vorstellungen des Kurfürsten mit einer Sandsteinterrasse umfangen, die von einer mit Putten und Vasen geschmückten Balustrade gefasst wird. An den Ecken der kreuzförmigen Insel rahmen insgesamt acht eingeschossige Kavaliershäuschen das heute als Museum genutzte Jagdschloss. Die Hatzen fanden im nahen Friedewald statt, der durch einen sogenannten Jagdstern für die Treibjagd erschlossen wurde.

The proceeding 16th century building with four circular towers, which are connected by four walls, predetermined the shape of what is today Moritzburg Palace. In 1703 the Saxonian Elector, August the Strong planned the modification of the building as a structure on an island of a lake. Toward this end, he ordered court architect, Matthäus Daniel Pöppelmann in 1716. Pöppelmann reoriented the existing structure and composed the horizontal projection around two courtyards of honor to make an H-shape. The architect raised two of the towers by two storeys, built the others from scratch and crowned them with the characteristic bonnets and lanterns. On the elector's suggestion, the central building was surrounded by a sandstone terrace, which was surrounded by a balustrade decorated with vases and putti. A total of eight single-storey guesthouses frame the hunting lodge on the corners of the cross-shaped island. The hunts took place in the near-by Friedewald, which was made accessible through a 'Jagdstern' (a 'star' of rides cut through a hunting forest or park) for the bateau. The palace is used as a museum today.

Zwinger

Dresden

Der Name dieser einzigartigen Anlage des Barock resultiert aus seiner Lage zwischen den Dresdner Befestigungsanlagen des Mittelalters und jenen des 16. Jahrhunderts. Der Architekt Matthäus Daniel Pöppelmann und der Bildhauer Balthasar Permoser errichteten von 1709 bis 1728 das mit zahlreichen figürlichen Allegorien geschmückte Garten- und Architektur-Ensemble für den sächsischen Kurfürsten August den Starken. Die leicht wirkenden Pavillonarchitekturen aus Elbsandstein umschließen einen annähernd quadratischen Hof, der auf zwei gegenüberliegenden Seiten in kleinere Höfe mit Segmentbogenschlüssen mündet. Eine besondere Sensation eröffnet der nördliche Treppenaufgang im Wallpavillon. Er führt zum sogenannten Nymphenbad, einem offenen Grottensaal mit einer Wasserkaskade, die in ein Becken mit wasserspeienden Nymphen und Tritonen fließt: Hier hat die im gesamten Zwinger spürbare Einheit von Architektur, Skulptur und Grün die Dimension des Hörbaren erreicht. Die nordöstliche Wand des Zwingers schloss Gottfried Semper von 1847 bis 1855 mit seiner kongenialen Gemäldegalerie.

The name of this one-of-a kind structure of the baroque period resulted from its situation between Dresden's fortification structures of the middle ages and those from the 16th century. Architect Matthäus Daniel Pöppelmann and sculptor Balthasar Permoser constructed the Zwinger for Elector of Saxony, August the Strong from 1709 to 1728. The garden and architectural ensemble is decorated with countless figurative allegories. The effortless pavilion architecture from Elbe sandstone surrounds an approximately square courtyard, which opens out on segmented bowed enclosures. Especially sensational is the northern stairwell in the wall pavilion, which leads into the 'Nymphenbad', an open grotto corridor with water cascades, and a pool with water-spraying tritons and nymphs: Unity and variability is noticeable throughout the entire Zwinger in architecture, sculpture, green spaces – and even sound. Gottfried Semper concluded the north-eastern wall of the Zwinger with his congenial gallery of paintings from 1847 to 1855.

Schloss Pillnitz

Dresden-Pillnitz

Ein Renaissanceanwesen des sächsischen Adels an der Elbe fiel 1694 an August den Starken, unter dessen Ägide in Pillnitz eine der reizendsten Schöpfungen des sächsischen Barock entstand. Er ließ von 1720 bis 1725 durch Matthäus Daniel Pöppelmann im Anschluss an die Renaissanceanlage das heutige Wasserpalais am Elbufer errichten. Dessen Pavillons sind fast durchgängig mit heiteren Chinoiserien bemalt, die thematisch mit der für kurfürstliche Feste verwendeten Architektur zusammenklingen, die ihrer Zeit gemäß ebenfalls fernöstliche Anregungen aufnimmt. Parallel dazu entstand ab 1723 das Bergpalais. Zugleich wurde die Gartenanlage unter anderem durch einen Spielgarten mit 16 Spielfeldern und ein Ringrenngebäude erweitert. König Friedrich August I. wählte Pillnitz schließlich zur Sommerresidenz und baute Park und Schloss weiter aus. Nach einem Brand 1818 entstand anstelle des Renaissancebaus das Neue Palais, das Wasser- und Bergpalais zusammenschließt.

A renaissance estate on the River Elbe belonging to a Saxon aristocratic family fell into the hands of August the Strong in 1694 under whose aegis Pillnitz became one of the most attractive creations of Saxony's baroque period. He commissioned Matthäus Daniel Pöppelmann from 1720 to 1725 to extend the renaissance estate on the bank of the River Elbe with the today's 'Water Palace'. The Water Palace's pavilions are covered with painted sanguine oriental figures, which thematically coincide with the architectural style of the palace incorporating then fashionable elements of the far-East. The 'Mountain Palace' was erected parallel to the pavilion from 1723 onward. The garden structure was expanded to include among others, a game garden with 16 game fields, and a ring race building. Finally, King Friedrich August I chose Pillnitz as his summer residence and expanded the garden and palace even further. After a fire in 1818, instead of the renaissance construction, the 'New Palace' was erected, which connects 'Water Palace' and 'Mountain Palace'.

Schloss Rammenau

Rammenau bei Bischofswerda, Kreis Bautzen

Die schöne Barockanlage wird dem bedeutenden Dresdner Architekten Johann Christoph Knöffel zugeschrieben. Den zweigeschossigen Sandsteinbau mit hohem Mansarddach, mit Cour d'honneur und nach einheitlichem Plan gestaltetem Wirtschaftshof ließ sich der kursächsische Kammerherr Ernst Ferdinand von Knoch von 1721 bis 1737 erbauen. Interessant ist die illusionistische Architekturmalerei, die die Fassaden des Hauptbaus mit Lisenen gliedert. Rittmeister Friedrich von Kleist, der das Rittergut Rammenau seit 1794 besaß, ließ den barocken Garten in einen Landschaftspark umwandeln. Aus dieser Umbauphase stammen auch die wertvollen Ledertapeten und Wandmalereien im Innern des Schlosses. Im Zuge der Bodenrefom in der sowjetischen Besatzungszone wurden 1945 die damaligen Besitzer enteignet. Seitdem befindet sich die mehrfach restaurierte Anlage in Staatsbesitz – heute als Hotel, Museum und Gedenkstätte für Johann Gottlieb Fichte, der im Ort Rammenau geboren wurde.

This lovely baroque estate is ascribed to one of Dresden's most distinguished architects, Johann Christoph Knöffel. The two-storey building, constructed from sandstone with a high mansard roof, forms a cour d'honneur. It was built by the Electorial Saxonian Chaimberlain, Ernst Ferdinand von Knoch between 1721 and 1737. Of special interest are the illusionist architectural paintings, which are arranged as pilaster strips on the façade of the main building. Cavalry Captain Friedrich von Kleist, who owned the manor of Rammenau since 1794, had the baroque gardens transformed into a scenic park. Priceless leather tapestries and wall murals inside the palace originate from this time period. In 1945 the then owners were dispossessed of the property with the land reform in the Soviet zone of occupation. Since that time, the restored estate had been in the ownership of the state. Today it is used as a hotel, museum and memorial for German philosopher, Johann Gottlieb Fichte, who was born in Rammenau.

Festung Königstein

Königstein bei Pirna, Sachsen

Wohl 1233 erstmals urkundlich erwähnt, entwickelte sich auf einem Tafelberg des Elbsandsteingebirges – 240 Meter über dem linken Elbufer – die größte Bergfestung Europas: Der Königstein gehörte ursprünglich zum Königreich Böhmen, ging aber im 15. Jahrhundert an den Markgrafen von Meißen. Kurfürst Christian I. von Sachsen ließ ihn im 16. Jahrhundert zur Festung ausbauen. In den kommenden Jahrhunderten wurde das Areal immer wieder den neuesten fortifikatorischen Bedürfnissen angepasst. Noch zwischen 1871 und 1895 erhielt die Festung Batteriewälle mit acht Geschützstellungen. Die Umwallung der gewaltigen Anlage, die militärisch weitgehend bedeutungslos blieb, hat heute 1,4 Kilometer Umfang und bis zu 40 Meter hohe Mauerteile. Bis 1922 war hier das sächsische Staatsgefängnis, in dem unter anderem Michail Bakunin, August Bebel und Frank Wedekind einsaßen. Zu DDR-Zeiten war der Königstein ein Jugendwerkhof für straffällige und auffällige Jugendliche. Heute ist der Königstein mit seinen Militär- und Zivilbauten aus vier Jahrhunderten ein militärhistorisches Freilichtmuseum von einzigartigem Rang.

Arguably the documents first mentioning Fortress Königstein date back to 1233. It was built up on a table mountain in the Elbe Sandstone Mountains (Saxon Switzerland) 240 meters over the left bank of the Elbe and is the largest mountain fortress in Europe. Königstein originally belonged to the Kingdom of Bohemia, but in the 15th century it was turned over to the Margrave of Meißen. Elector Christian I of Saxony had it expanded into a fortress in the 16th century. In the following century it was continually updated with the latest requirements for fortification. Still between 1871 and 1895 battery ramparts with eight canon settings were added to the fortress. The enclosure of the enormous construction, which remained widely unused for military defense, today has a circumference of 1.4 kilometers and portions of the fortification wall are 40 meters high. Until 1922 it served as the state prison of Saxony. Among those incarcerated in the prison were Michail Bakunin, August Bebel and Frank Wedekind and, in the former East Germany, juvenile delinquents and wayward youth were sent there as well. Today with its military and civil history of four hundred years Königstein is a one-of-a-kind open-air museum.

Schloss Augustusburg

Augustusburg, Landkreis Freiberg, Erzgebirge

Auf dem 516 Meter hohen Schellenberg im nördlichen Erzgebirge ließ Kurfürst August I. von Sachsen 1568 bis 1572 anstelle einer älteren Burganlage ein monumentales Schloss in Idealformen der italienischen Renaissance errichten. Die nach Ansicht des Bauherrn schleppende Bauausführung durch den Leipziger Bürgermeister Hieronymus Lotter führte zu einem Wechsel der Bauleitung. Obwohl Lotter schon 1570 mit zeitweise 750 Arbeitskräften „23 gemach vorferttiget mit gemelde", wurde Rochus Guerini Graf zu Lynar mit der Oberaufsicht beauftragt; die Bauleitung übernahm Erhard van der Meer. Trotz späterer Umbauten hat die Vierflügelanlage, deren Entwurf häufig dem architektonisch interessierten Landesherrn selbst zugeschrieben wird, ihr ursprüngliches Aussehen bewahrt: Grundriss wie Aufriss bauen auf dem Modul des Quadrats auf und zeigen vollendete Symmetrie und proportionale Ausgewogenheit – ein Musterbeispiel für die Umsetzung der auf dem antik-römischen Architekturschriftsteller Vitruv aufbauenden Architekturtheorie der Renaissance. Heute ist Augustusburg Jugendherberge und birgt mehrere kleine Museen.

Elector August of Saxony built a monumental palace in the idealized architectonic forms of the Italian renaissance from 1568 to 1572 atop the 516 meter high Schellenberg in the northern Erzgebirge instead of an old castle. From the point of view of the awarding authority, the contractor, Hieronymus Lotter from Leipzig, the execution of the construction work was sluggish, which lead to a change of construction leadership. Although Lotter already in 1570 had, at times, as many as 750 laborers, Rochus Guerini Graf zu Lynar was entrusted with the oversight and the site management was overtaken by Erhard van der Meer. The four-storey estate, whose blueprint was often accredited to the architecturally-interested Sovereign Lord himself, despite later renovations, conserved its original appearance. Ground plan and façades were based on the module of the square and demonstrate perfected symmetry and proportional balance – an ideal example for the architectural theory of the renaissance which is based on the works of the ancient Roman writer and architect Vitruvius. Today Augustusburg offers a youth hostel and a row of museums.

Burg Scharfenstein

Drebach-Scharfenstein, Erzgebirge

Um 1250 wurde die Burg auf einem Bergsporn des Erzgebirges als Sitz der Herren von Waldenburg auf Wolkenstein errichtet. Nach mehreren Besitzerwechseln erwarb Heinrich von Einsiedel 1492 die charakteristische Anlage mit einem Witwen-, Gesellschafts- und Wohnflügel und hohem, rundem Bergfried. 1921 brannte Scharfenstein nieder. Der Architekt Bodo Ebhardt baute die Burg nach historischem Vorbild wieder auf. Seit 1931 gehörte sie einem sächsischen Industriellen, ab 1950 war sie zuerst Kinderheim, dann „Jugendwerkhof". Nach der Übernahme durch den Freistaat Sachsen 1993 richtete man in der restaurierten Burg Scharfenstein ein Weihnachts- und Spielzeugmuseum mit erzgebirgischem Kunsthandwerk sowie ein Museum für den legendären Wildschütz Karl Stülpner ein.

Around the year 1250 the castle was erected upon a cliff of the Erzgebirge as the official residence of the Lords of Waldenburg on Wolkenstein. After many changes in ownership, it was purchased by Heinrich von Einsiedel in 1492. It is a characteristical estate that includes a widow's wing, a reception wing, a wing for living, and a high, round donjon. Scharfenstein Castle burned to the ground in 1921. Architect Bodo Ebhardt rebuilt the castle according to the historic model. Beginning in 1931 it belonged to an industrialist from Saxony, and from 1950 onward it was first a home for children and then a 'youth operation center'. After it was overtaken by the federal state of Saxony in 1993, the restored Scharfenstein Castle houses a Christmas Museum, and a Toy Museum with arts and craft items from the Erzgebirge and also a museum of a legendary Erzgebirgian poacher, Karl Stülpner.

Stiftsschloss Quedlinburg

Quedlinburg, Sachsen-Anhalt

Auf einem Bergplateau oberhalb der heutigen Stadt ließ König Heinrich I. 922 eine Reichsburg erbauen. Seine Witwe Mathilde gründete dort nach seinem Tod (936) ein Stift für adelige Damen. Die ehemalige Burgkapelle wurde zur romanischen Stiftskirche St. Servatius ausgebaut. Die drei Flügel des heutigen Stiftsschlosses entstanden in der Renaissance (seit 1521). Die Äbtissin bewohnte den im Norden gelegenen Residenzflügel mit seinen Zwerchhäusern und einem Treppenturm mit welscher Haube (1557/1559). Aus dem 18. Jahrhundert stammen die den Hof umschließende Fachwerkgalerie, die Neue Abtei sowie mit Stukkaturen im Régencestil gestaltete Repräsentationsräume wie der Blaue Saal oder der Thronsaal. Vom ehemaligen Schlosspark bietet sich ein schöner Rundblick über Quedlinburg mit seinem einzigartigen Bestand historischer Fachwerkhäuser.

King Heinrich I built a castle for the empire atop a mountain plateau overlooking the today's city in 922. After his death in 936, his widow Mathilde founded a convent for aristocratic women. The former castle chapel was rebuilt to become the romanesque convent church of Saint Servatius. The three wings of the convent palace were erected in the renaissance (1521). The abbess occupied the northern-lying residential wing with its gable lucarnes and a stair tower with a bulbous dome (1557/1559). The courtyard is surrounded by a framework gallery, which dates from the 18th century as well as the so called 'New Abbey' and stucco works in Régence style in the Blue Hall and the Throne Room. The former palace gardens offer a lovely panoramic view over Quedlinburg with its unique historical framework houses.

Wartburg

Eisenach, Thüringen

Schauplatz des legendären „Sängerkriegs" mit Walther von der Vogelweide und Wolfram von Eschenbach, Wohnort der Elisabeth von Thüringen, Zuflucht Martin Luthers und Kulisse der Wartburgfeste der deutschen Burschenschaften: Die Burganlage auf einem steil abfallenden Felsplateau oberhalb des thüringischen Eisenach galt schon im 19. Jahrhundert wegen ihrer historischen Bedeutung als Nationaldenkmal. Von der um 1067 gegründeten, im 12. und 13. Jahrhundert ausgebauten Abschnittsburg mit ursprünglich vier jeweils durch Befestigungen voneinander getrennten Teilen sind noch Vor- und Hauptburg erhalten. Bedeutendster aus dem Mittelalter überkommener Teil ist der Palas mit der angrenzenden Doppelkapelle aus der Mitte des 12. Jahrhunderts. In weiten Teilen ist die Burg indes eine Rekonstruktion des 19. Jahrhunderts – Großherzog Carl Alexander von Sachsen-Weimar und Eisenach (1818–1901) beauftragte 1849 den Gießener Architekten Hubert von Ritgens mit der Wiederherstellung der historischen Stätte nach eigenen Entwürfen. Nach wie vor jedoch gilt die heute museal genutzte Wartburg als Inbegriff der deutschen Burg.

Scene of the legendary 'Sängerkrieg' ('War of the Minstrels') with Walther von der Vogelweide and Wolfram von Eschenbach, residence of Elisabeth of Hungary von Thüringen, refuge of Martin Luther, and set of the Wartburg Festival of German Student Fraternities: the castle structure atop a steeply sloping rocky plateau over the city of Eisenach in Thuringia was already a national landmark in the 19th century because of its historical significance. Founded in 1067, with additional portions added to fortify the original four separate sections in the 12th and 13th century, the front castle and the main castle have been sustained. The Great Hall with the adjoining two-storey chapel from the middle of the 12th century is the most important surviving portion from the Middle Ages. Other parts of the castle are a reconstruction for the 19th century. Grand Duke Carl Alexander of Sachsen-Weimar and Eisenach (1818–1901) commissioned the architect Hubert von Ritgens of Giessen to reconstruct the historical location based on his own design in 1849. As before, Wartburg, which is now used as a museum, embodies the definition of the German castle.

Schloss Augustusburg

Brühl bei Köln

Schloss Augustusburg in Brühl bei Köln war die Lieblingsresidenz des Kölner Kurfürsten und Erzbischofs Clemens August von Wittelsbach. Es zählt zu den bedeutenden Schöpfungen des Rokoko in Deutschland. Der westfälische Baumeister Johann Conrad Schlaun begann 1725 mit der Errichtung des Schlosses auf den Ruinen einer mittelalterlichen Wasserburg. Unter dem französischen Hofbaumeister François de Cuvilliès erhielt es seine Ausgestaltung als herausragende Residenz dieser Zeit. Das weithin bekannte Prunktreppenhaus – „eine hinreißende Schöpfung voller Dynamik und Eleganz" – entwarf Balthasar Neumann. Ab 1949 war Schloss Augustusburg jahrzehntelang Repräsentationssitz des Bundespräsidenten und der Bundesregierung. 1984 wurde die Gesamtanlage – Schloss Augustusburg mit der axial verbundenen *maison de plaisance* Falkenlust, der rekonstruierten barocken Gartenanlage und dem von Peter Joseph Lenné gestalteten Landschaftsgarten – in die Liste des Weltkulturerbes eingetragen. Im Besitz des Landes Nordrhein-Westfalen, sind Schlösser und Gärten der Öffentlichkeit zugänglich.

Palace Augustusburg is located in Brühl near Cologne and was the preferred residence of the Elector and Arch-bishop of Cologne, Clemens August von Wittelsbach. It belongs to the most prestigious rococo creations in Germany. The contractor, Johann Conrad Schlaun of Westphalia, began the construction of the palace in 1725 on top of the ruins of a medieval moated castle. Under the direction of the architect of the French Court, François de Cuvilliès, it received its exterior design as an outstanding residence of the time period. The well-known grandiose staircase was conceptualized by Balthasar Neumann, by a critique's word 'a ravishing creation full of vitality and elegance'. Following 1949, Palace Augustusburg served for decades as the representational seat of the Federal President and Federal Government. The entire estate, including Augustusburg Palace, the connecting *maison de plaisance* Falkenlust, the reconstructed Baroque garden, and the scenic landscape gardens designed by Peter Joseph Lenné have been added to the list of World-Culture Heritage Sights. Owned by the state of North-Rhine Westphalia, the gardens and palaces are open to the public.

Schloss Arenfels

Bad Hönningen, Mittelrhein

Das Schloss über dem Touristenparadies Bad Hönningen ist das Resultat der Umgestaltung eines Renaissancebaus der Grafen von Isenburg und von Wied aus der zweiten Hälfte des 16. Jahrhunderts. Architekt war der Kölner Dombaumeister Ernst Friedrich Zwirner, der gegen die Absicht seines Bauherrn Reichsgraf Ludolf Friedrich von Westerholt-Gysenberg weitreichende Eingriffe vornahm: Er versah die Dreiflügelanlage über dem Rhein, die auf Resten 1259 erstmals erwähnter Vorgängerbauten steht, ab 1852 mit gotisierenden Treppengiebeln, errichtete den runden Bergfried neu und erhöhte die Treppentürme, so dass sich das pittoreske Bild eines auf einer hohen Terrasse stehenden Idealbaus des späten Mittelalters ergab. Nach Kriegs- und Umweltschäden wurde der Bau mehrfach, zuletzt 2000 bis 2003, restauriert. Heute dient dieses herausragende Beispiel rheinischer Neogotik gastronomischen Zwecken sowie den Veranstaltungen einer Privatakademie.

The palace overlooking the tourist paradise of Bad Hönningen is the result of the remodeling of a renaissance building, which belonged to Count von Isenburg and Count von Wied from the second half of the 16th century. The architect was Ernst Friedrich Zwirner, the construction manager of the Cologne Cathedral in the 19th century, who against the intentions of his awarding authority, Count of the Empire Ludolf Friedrich von Westerholt-Gysenberg, undertook a far-reaching intervention in the project: He supplied the three-wing construction, which stood upon the remains of the pre-existing building first mentioned in 1259, with gothic crowstep gables from 1852 onwards. Zwirner built a new round donjon, and heightened the stair towers to create the picturesque image of an ideal medieval structure standing on a high terrace above the River Rhine. Due to war and environmental damage, the building has been restored many times, the last of which was from 2000 to 2003. Today this outstanding example of the neo-gothic period of the Rhine serves for gastronomic purposes as well as for events for a private academy.

Schloss Stolzenfels

Koblenz-Stolzenfels, Mittelrhein

Der Trierer Erzbischof Arnold II. von Isenburg ließ zum Schutz des Rheinzolls von 1242 bis 1259 eine Burg errichten, von der ein fünfseitiger Bergfried erhalten ist. Arnolds Nachfolger Kuno II. und Werner von Falkenstein erweiterten den Bau im Spätmittelalter beträchtlich. Im Pfälzischen Erbfolgekrieg von 1689 wurde er wie viele andere Burgen am Rhein zerstört. Die Ruine machte die Stadt Koblenz dem späteren preußischen König Friedrich Wilhelm IV. zum Geschenk, der sie 1836 bis 1842 von Karl Friedrich Schinkel und Friedrich August Stüler wieder aufbauen ließ. Die romantische Lage in der Nähe eines Wasserfalls am steilen Rheinufer, die Mischung aus denkmalpflegerischer Erhaltung des mittelalterlichen Baus und seiner schöpferischen Weiterentwicklung durch Schinkel, der effektvoll inszenierte Blick auf das Rheintal und die vollständig erhaltenen Interieurs machen das museal genutzte Schloss Stolzenfels zu einem Hauptwerk der Romantik. Seit 2002 ist es Teil des UNESCO-Weltkulturerbes „Oberes Mittelrheintal".

The Arch-bishop of Trier, Arnold II of Isenburg had a castle built from 1242 until 1259 to protect his tariffs on the River Rhine. The five-sided donjon still exists today. Arnold's successors, Kuno II and Werner von Falkenstein extensively expanded the building in the late-Middle Ages. Like many other castles of the Rhine, it was destroyed in 1689 during the War of the Grand Alliance. The city of Koblenz gave the ruins to the future King Friedrich Wilhelm IV of Prussia who added different parts to the palace from 1836 to 1842, lead by Karl Friedrich Schinkel and Friedrich August Stüler. The romantic environment in the near of a waterfall on a cliff bank overlooking the River Rhine, the carefully conserved medieval structure and the completely preserved historistic interior, make Palace Stolzenfels, which is now used as a museum, a major work of the romantic period. Since 2002 it has been part of the UNESCO World Cultural Heritage Sight 'Upper Middle Rhine Valley'.

Marksburg

Braubach, Mittelrhein

Die einzige unzerstörte Höhenburg am Rhein entstand kurz nach 1200. Unter dem Namen „Burg Braubach" gehörte sie den Herren von Eppstein, ab 1283 denen von Katzenelnbogen. Aus dieser Zeit sind die annähernd im Dreieck angelegten Schildmauern der Hochburg, der Palas, der Bergfried auf quadratischem Grundriss und der Kapellenturm erhalten. Graf Johann II. von Katzenelnbogen ließ die Burg um 1350 in Formen der Gotik zu einer repräsentativen Wohnanlage umbauen, die 1437 – nach der Stiftung einer Markuskapelle – ihren heutigen Namen erhielt. Dieser Umbau prägt das Aussehen der Marksburg bis heute, sie gilt als weitgehende authentische Anlage des späten Mittelalters. Ab 1479 hessisch, verlor die Marksburg durch die als neue Residenz nahebei erbaute Philippsburg an Bedeutung. Um 1900 gelangte die inzwischen verfallene Burg in den Besitz der Deutschen Burgenvereinigung, die dort heute ihre Geschäftsräume unterhält. Im japanischen Ueno wurde in den 1990er Jahren eine originalgetreue Kopie der Marksburg errichtet.

The single undestroyed elevated castle on the Rhine River was built shortly after 1200. Under the name 'Castle Braubach' it belonged to the Lords von Eppstein. After 1283 it came to the Lords von Katzenelnbogen. The triangularly laid shield walls of the elevated fortress, the great hall, the donjon on a quadratic ground plan, and the chapel tower have been built in this time period. Count Johann II. von Katzenelnbogen renovated the castle as a representative living area in the Gothic style around 1350. It is from the donation of a Markus chapel in 1437 that the castle received its current name. This renovation has determined the external appearance of the castle until today. The castle is considered to be a vastly authentic construction of the late Middle Ages. Marksburg lost significance through the construction nearby of the new residence Philippsburg in 1479. Around 1900 the castle, which had in the meantime fell into disrepair, landed in the hands of the German Castles Association, which today has its official offices there. An exact replica of Marksburg was built in the Japanese city of Ueno in the 1990s.

Burg Sterrenberg und Burg Liebenstein

Kamp-Bornhofen, Mittelrhein

Die beiden einander dicht gegenüberliegenden Burgruinen bei Bornhofen werden die „Feindlichen Brüder" genannt. Die gleichermaßen als Verteidigungsanlage wie als Sicherung des Zolls bei Bornhofen fungierende Burg Sterrenberg wird schon 1034 als Reichsburg erwähnt. Im 14. Jahrhundert fiel sie an den Trierer Erzbischof, der eine Burg Liebenstein sehr nahe kommende zweite Schildmauer errichten ließ: Sie wurde möglicherweise Ausgangspunkt der Sage von den „feindlichen Brüdern". Weil die ab 1353 erbaute, ebenfalls trierische Burg Maus eine bessere strategische Lage besaß, verlor Burg Sterrenberg ihre Funktion. Schon 1456 galt sie als „baufällig", im 16. Jahrhundert war sie unbewohnt.

Burg Liebenstein entstand wohl im 13. Jahrhundert als Vorburg von Burg Sterrenberg. Graf Albrecht von Löwenstein befestigte zwischen 1284 und 1290 die Anlage gegen den auf Sperrenberg ansässigen Onkel seiner Gattin. Sie blieb als Ganerbenburg Familienbesitz: Zeitweise lebten bis zu zehn Teilfamilien auf der Burg, die jeweils eigene Wohn- und Befestigungsanlagen unterhielten. Auch Burg Liebenstein verfiel im 16. Jahrhundert. Beide Ruinen wurden in den 1970er Jahren restauriert und zu gastronomischen Zwecken ausgebaut.

The two castle ruins, lying opposite of each other near Bornhofen are called the 'Feindlichen Brüder' ('enemy brothers'). Sterrenberg functioned as a defensive structure and as security for customs near Bornhofen at the same time. Already in 1034 it was mentioned as a castle of the Holy Roman Empire. In the 14th century it fell into the hands of the Arch-bishop of Trier, who built a second shield wall very near to Liebenstein Castle. This was probably the starting point of the 'Feindliche Brüder' saga. Since 1353 Burg Maus of Trier was located in a strategically better location and Sterrenberg was stripped of its purpose then.

Between 1284 and 1290 Count Albrecht von Löwenstein fortified the faubourg of Sterrenberg as a safe guard against his wife's uncle, who owned the main castle. Sterrenberg remained in family possession as a so called Ganerbenburg (a castle which is owned by different families). From time to time, as many as 10 family members, who respectively supported their own residential and fortification constructions, resided in the castle. Castle Liebenstein also fell into disrepair in the 16th century. Both ruins have been restored in the 1970's and rebuilt as restaurants.

Deuernburg/Burg Maus

St. Goarshausen-Wellmich, Mittelrhein

Der Trierer Erzbischof Boemund II. ließ unter dem Namen „Peterseck" oder auch Deuernburg in Wellmich eine Burgfeste errichten. Die erste Phase des Baus datiert in die Jahre 1353 bis 1357, unter Boemunds Nachfolgern Kuno II. von Falkenstein und Werner von Falkenstein wurde die Anlage bis 1388 fertiggestellt. Das beeindruckende Ensemble in strategisch ausgezeichneter Lage diente zeitweise sogar als Residenz der Trierer. Der Name „Burg Maus" stammt wohl aus späterer Zeit, als die Grafen von Katzenelnbogen in der Nähe die konkurrierende Burg Neukatzenelnbogen – auch „Burg Katz" genannt – errichtet hatten. Ihr heutiges Aussehen verdankt die zwischenzeitlich auf Abriss verkaufte Burg Maus indes dem Wiederaufbau des Architekten Wilhelm Gärtner zwischen 1900 und 1906, der ein imposantes Idealbild der bergfriedbekrönten Burganlage rekonstruierte. In Burg Maus ist heute ein Jagdvogelhof untergebracht, wo regelmäßig Flugvorführungen stattfinden.

Arch-bishop Boemund II of Trier built a fortress in Wellmich that was called by the names of 'Peterseck' ('Peter's Corner') or Deuernburg. The first building phase dates back to between 1353 and 1357. The structure was completed under Boemund's successors, Kuno II von Falkenstein and Werner von Falkenstein in 1388. The impressive ensemble in a strategically excellent location actually served in part as the official residence in Trier. The name 'Burg Maus' ('Mouse Castle') stems from a later time period: when the Counts of Katzenelnbogen constructed a rival fortress, Neukatzenelnbogen Castle (also called 'Cat Castle') nearby. The current look of Burg Maus is thanks to architect Wilhelm Gärtner who rebuilt it between 1900 and 1906 who held a commanding ideal of how to reconstruct the donjon-crowned castle structure. Today Burg Maus hosts an aviary that is home to falcons and eagles, and flight demonstrations are regularly staged for visitors.

Burg Stahleck

Bacharach, Mittelrhein

Die Burg bei Bacharach am Rhein wird erstmals 1135 erwähnt. Sie bildete zusammen mit der gegenüberliegenden Burg Gutenfels bei Kaub die nördliche Sicherungslinie der Pfalz. Aus alten Darstellungen lässt sich eine monumentale Anlage mit zentralem Bergfried und rheinseitigem Palas erschließen. Sie war mit dem – heute noch weitgehend erhaltenen – Befestigungsring der Stadt verbunden. Im Pfälzischen Erbfolgekrieg 1689 wurde die Burg von französischen Soldaten gesprengt. Die Ruine war Besitz des preußischen Kronprinzen Friedrich Wilhelm, der sie 1825 seiner Gattin überließ. Anders als bei anderen Burgruinen entlang des Rheins verzichtete das Königshaus auf einen romantisierenden Wiederaufbau der wenigen Reste. 1925 errichtete man auf den Ruinen eine Jugendherberge. Als solche dient Stahleck noch heute.

The castle on the River Rhine near Bacharach was first mentioned in 1135. Together with Castle Gutenfels located near Kaub, the two castles formed the northern fortification of the Palatinate territory. Ancient illustrations show a monumental fortress with a central donjon and a 'palas' facing the River Rhine. The fortress was meant to combine with a fortification ring around the city, which today remains extensively preserved. In 1689, during the War of the Grand Alliance, the castle was exploded by French soldiers. The ruins became the property of Crown-prince Friedrich Wilhelm, who left them to his wife in 1825. In contrast to other castle ruins along the River Rhine, the royal dynasty avoided a romantic reconstruction of the few remains of the castle. A youth hostel was constructed from the ruins in 1925, and Stahleck remains a hostel even today.

Burg Ehrenfels und Mäuseturm

Rüdesheim, Mittelrhein

Auf der um 983 erbauten Hangburg lebte um 1150 ein Ritter namens Widerscholl. Um 1211 ließ Philipp von Bolanden die Burg mit einer von zwei Ecktürmen flankierten 20 Meter hohen Schildmauer ausbauen und im Norden durch einen Burggraben sichern. Später wurde Ehrenfels von Kurmainzern besetzt und seit Mitte des 13. Jahrhunderts als Zollstation genutzt. Zur Burg gehörte ein um 1270 auf einer Insel im Rhein erbauter Wehr- und Wachturm, der „Mäuseturm" genannt wurde. Vorgängerbauten hatte es schon in römischer Zeit gegeben. Im Pfälzischen Erbfolgekrieg wurden Burg und Turm 1689 von französischem Militär weitgehend zerstört. Den Mäuseturm am „Binger Loch" ließ Friedrich Wilhelm IV. von 1856 bis 1858 im neugotischen Stil als preußische Grenzmarke wiedererrichten. Die an einem Wanderweg zwischen Rüdesheim und Assmannshausen gelegene Burgruine besteht heute aus der Schildmauer sowie Resten von Torbau und Palas.

In 1150 a knight named Widerscholl lived in the slope castle, which was built around 983. In approximately 1211, Philipp von Bolanden flanked the castle with two corner towers and a shield wall that was 20 meters high. It was also protected by a moat to the north. Ehrenfels was later owned by Kurmainz and was used as a duty station in the middle of the 13th century. A military watchtower, called the 'Mäuseturm' ('Mice Tower') built around 1270 on an island in the River Rhine belonged to the castle, too. There were already previous buildings there from the time of the Roman Empire. The castle and tower were mostly destroyed by the French military in 1689 during the War of the Grand Alliance. From 1856 to 1858, Friedrich Wilhelm IV had the Mäuseturm rebuilt in Neo-Gothic style to serve as a Prussian landmark at the famous river bend 'Binger Loch'. Today, the ruins of the castle, shield wall, as well as the rest of the gate and the great hall still stand on a beautiful hiking path between Rüdesheim and Assmannshausen.

Schloss Saarbrücken

Saarbrücken, Saarland

An der Stelle einer mittelalterlichen Burg errichteten die Fürsten von Saarbrücken zwischen 1602 und 1617 ein um mehrere Höfe angeordnetes Renaissanceschloss. Diese Anlage, 1677 zerstört und bis 1696 wiederaufgebaut, wurde von 1738 bis 1748 durch einen vollständigen dreiflügligen Neubau nach Plänen des nassau-saarbrückischen Generalbaudirektors Friedrich Joachim Stengel ersetzt. Der kunstsinnige Fürst Wilhelm Heinrich integrierte seit den 1740er Jahren den Schlossneubau in umfangreiche Maßnahmen zur Stadterweiterung, die ebenfalls Stengel plante. 1793 wurde der Nordflügel des Schlosses niedergebrannt. Sein Wiederaufbau in anderen Dimensionen ab 1810 leitete einen kontinuierlichen Substanzverlust des bedeutenden Rokokobaus ein, der im Abriss des Mittelteils des Corps de Logis gipfelte. Der Neubau des Mittelrisaliten als Stahl-Glas-Pavillon in postmoderner Formsprache durch den Kölner Architekten Gottfried Böhm interpretierte 1989 den Altbau neu.

The Sovereigns of Saarbrücken erected their renaissance palace around multiple courtyards between 1602 and 1617 in the place of a medieval castle. This arrangement, destroyed in 1677 and reconstructed until 1696, was replaced by the plan for a completely new three-winged construction created by General Building Director of Nassau-Saarbrücken, Friedrich Joachim Stengel, from 1738 until 1748. The Sovereign Wilhelm Heinrich who was interested in the arts integrated the rebuilding of the palace in a large-scale expansion of the city from the 1740s onward, which was also planned by Stengel. In 1793 the North-wing of the palace was burned. Its reconstruction with smaller dimensions from 1810, lead to a continuous asset erosion of the prominent rococo structure, which peaked with the demolition of the mid-section of the Corps de Logis. The new construction, by architect Gottfried Böhm of Cologne of the central projection as a steel and glass pavilion was created as a post-modern statement, which reinterpreted the old building anew in 1989.

Heidelberger Schloss

Heidelberg, Neckar / Baden-Württemberg

Bereits 1225 urkundlich als „castrum" erwähnt, erlebte das Schloss in Heidelberg zwischen dem 13. und 18. Jahrhundert als Residenz der Kurfürsten von der Pfalz eine wechselvolle Geschichte. Die bedeutendsten Bauten des Schlosses stammen aus der Renaissance, der berühmteste ist der ruinöse Ottheinrichsbau, den Kurfürst Otto Heinrich ab 1556 errichten ließ. Im Dreißigjährigen Krieg eroberte General Tilly 1622 Stadt und Schloss: Die berühmte, im Schloss bewahrte Bibliotheca Palatina, heute im Vatikan, wurde nach Italien verbracht. Den Verheerungen und Zerstörungen folgten mehrere Wiederaufbauphasen. Bereits im 19. Jahrhundert war Heidelberg für seine romantische Schlossruine weltberühmt. Um 1900 kam es über Art und Weise der Restaurierungen und das Maß der geplanten Restaurierung zu einem grundsätzlichen Richtungsstreit in Kunstgeschichte, Architektur und Denkmalpflege über die Möglichkeit baulicher Rekonstruktionen – vollständig wurde das Heidelberger Schloss nie mehr aufgebaut.

First mentioned in 1255 as a 'Castrum', Heidelberg Palace served as the official residence of the Elector of Pfalz between the 13th and 18th century and survived an ever-changing history. The most important sections of the palace stem from the renaissance, the most famous is the ruinous Ottheinrichsbau, which the Elector Otto Heinrich had built from 1556 onwards. During the Thirty Years' War in 1622 General Tilly captured the city and the palace. The famous Bibliotheca Palatina (a German library of the renaissance) was carried to Italy, and now rests in the Vatican. Subsequent devastation and destruction was followed by multiple reconstructions. Already in the 19th century Heidelberg was world-renowned for its romantic castle ruins. Around 1900 a lot of measures were taken toward restoring the palace. The degree of the planned restoration lead to a discussion between art historians, architects and preservationists concerning the reconstruction of ruined historical buildings. In the end, the palace of Heidelberg was never again completely rebuilt.

Schloss Schwetzingen

Schwetzingen, Rhein-Neckar-Kreis

1350 als Wasserburg erstmals erwähnt, diente Schloss Schwetzingen in den folgenden Jahrhunderten dem pfälzischen Hof als Jagdschloss. Im Dreißigjährigen Krieg wurde es verwüstet und anschließend wieder aufgebaut. Nach einer erneuten Brandkatastrophe schloss Kurfürst Johann Wilhelm den neuerlichen Wiederaufbau 1701 ab. Weitere Umgestaltungen folgten im Lauf der Zeit: Mit dem Anbau der Communsbauten zur Stadt hin erhielt das Schwetzinger Schloss den Charakter einer Dreiflügelanlage, die einen Ehrenhof umschließt. Ab 1752 wurden die großzügigen Schlossgärten angelegt. Die französische geprägte Gartenanlage des Architekten Nicolas de Pigage, die in einzigartiger Weise im 20. Jahrhundert rekonstruiert wurde, ergänzte etwas später Ludwig von Sckell durch einen englischen Landschaftsgarten. Im 1752 erbauten Schlosstheater finden heute die „Schwetzinger Festspiele" statt.

First mentioned as a moated castle in 1350, the palace of Schwetzingen served in the following centuries as a hunting palace for the Palatine court. During the Thirty Years' War it was ravaged and in the end, finally rebuilt. After a devastating fire catastrophe Elector Johann Wilhelm decided to rebuild it anew in 1701. Further modification followed with the passage of time. With the addition of buildings facing the city, the palace adapted the character of a three-wing estate, which encircles a court of honor. The singular French embossed garden composition by architect Nicolas de Pigage, which was added since 1752, has been reconstructed in the 20th century. Shortly afterward it was supplemented by an English scenic garden designed by Ludwig von Sckell. The palace theater, built in 1752, today houses the 'Schwetzinger Festspiele' ('Pageants of Schwetzingen').

Schloss Ludwigsburg

Ludwigsburg, Baden-Württemberg

Zwischen 1704 und 1733 entstand unter Herzog Eberhard Ludwig von Württemberg die Ludwigsburger Residenz als eine der größten barocken Schlossbauten Deutschlands. Dem zunächst im Norden des Areals errichteten mächtigen Hauptbau fügte man später den Jagd- und Spielpavillon sowie weitere Verbindungsgalerien hinzu, so dass eine Dreiflügelanlage mit nach Süden offenem Ehrenhof entstand. Durch zusätzliche Bauten wurde die bestehende Anlage im Laufe der langen Bauzeit geschlossen. Schloss Ludwigsburg umfasst 452 Räume, zwei Kirchen und ein Theater. Die Residenz ist auf drei Seiten von einer großen Parkanlage umgeben, die 1954 zur 250-Jahr-Feier des Schlosses in historischer Form neu angelegt wurde. Heute beherbergt der Bau mehrere Museen: Originale Raumausstattungen zeigen mit Gestaltungsformen des Barock, Rokoko, Klassizismus und Empire die unterschiedlichen Auffassungen verschiedener Epochen.

The residence of Ludwigsburg came into existence between 1704 and 1733 under Duke Eberhard Ludwig von Württemberg as one of Germany's largest baroque palace estates. A hunting and gambling pavilion and other attached galleries were added to the estate's enormous main building so that a three-wing construction with an open court of honor facing to the south was created. Through the addition of further wings, the existing courtyard was closed through the course of a long period of construction. Ludwigsburg Palace consists of 452 rooms, two churches and one theater. The residence is surrounded by a large park on three sides, which for its 250-year anniversary was reconstructed according to its original design in 1954. Today the building houses a number of museums. Original room interiors in baroque, rococo, classicist and Empire style show the different notions of various epochs.

Neues Schloss

Stuttgart

Als eine der letzten Barockresidenzen wurde das Neue Schloss für Herzog Carl Eugen von Württemberg in unmittelbarer Nachbarschaft zum Alten Schloss in der Mitte Stuttgarts errichtet. Die Grundsteinlegung erfolgte 1746. Bis zur Mitte des 18. Jahrhunderts waren der Corps de logis und der Gartenflügel vollendet, der Stadtflügel stand im Rohbau. Wegen der Verlegung seiner Residenz nach Ludwigsburg ließ Carl Eugen schließlich die Arbeiten am Neuen Schloss abbrechen. 1775, nach der Rückkehr des Herzogs, begannen Instandsetzungsarbeiten, die sich bis zur Fertigstellung der Anlage im Jahr 1807 hinzogen. Nach dem Ende der Monarchie 1918 ging das Neue Schloss in den Besitz des Landes Baden-Württemberg über. Im Zweiten Weltkrieg fast völlig zerstört, wurde es zwischen 1958 und 1964 wieder aufgebaut. Heute dient es der baden-württembergischen Landesregierung als Sitz von Finanz- und Kultusministerium.

The New Palace for Duke Carl Eugen von Württemberg was built in the center of Stuttgart in close proximity to the Old Palace, as one of the final Baroque official residences. The foundation stone was laid in 1746. In the middle of the 18th century the Corps de logis and the garden wing were completed, but the city wing remained only the shell of the future building. Because of the relocation of his official residence to Ludwigsburg, Carl Eugen finally decided to discontinue the building of the New Palace. In 1775, after the return of the duke, restoration work began, which was prolonged until the final completion of the structure in 1807. After the end of the monarchy in 1918, the New Palace became the property of the state of Baden-Württemberg. Though nearly completely destroyed in the Second World War, it was rebuilt between 1958 and 1964. It now serves as the official seats of the Ministry of Finance and the Ministry of Education and Cultural Affairs for the state government of Baden-Württemberg.

Burg Hohenzollern

Bisingen-Zimmern, Schwäbische Alb

Burg Hohenzollern war die Stammburg des Fürstengeschlechts der Hohenzollern. Die mittelalterliche Burg wurde um 1423 vollständig zerstört, ein Neubau 1454 in Angriff genommen. Obwohl im Dreißigjährigen Krieg zur Festung ausgebaut, wurde die Burg im Laufe der Zeit mehrfach schwer beschädigt und verfiel zusehends. Seit 1819 plante der damalige Kronprinz und spätere König Friedrich Wilhelm IV. einen Wiederaufbau. In ihrer heutigen Form ist die Burg ein Bauwerk des Berliner Architekten Friedrich August Stüler. 1850 legte man feierlich den Grundstein, im Jahre 1867 wurde der Bau unter Wilhelm I. vollendet und eingeweiht. Die Burg ist nach wie vor in Privatbesitz. Seit Mitte der 1950er Jahre wird Burg Hohenzollern auch für Ferienaufenthalte bedürftiger Berliner Kinder genutzt.

Castle Hohenzollern was the family seat of the line of Hohenzollern princes. The medieval castle was completely destroyed in 1423, with the onset of reconstruction in 1454. Even though the castle was expanded into a fortress during the Thirty Years' War, through the passage of time it was heavily damaged and noticeably decayed. In 1819 the then Hohenzollern Crown-prince, who became King Friedrich Wilhelm IV of Prussia planned a reconstruction of the castle. In its present form, it is the work of the king's architect, Friedrich August Stüler. The cornerstone was ceremoniously laid in 1850, and the construction was completed and inaugurated under the later 'Kaiser' Wilhelm I in 1867. As before, the castle is now owned by the Hohenzollern dynasty. Since the mid-fifties, Hohenzollern Castle has also been used as a vacation destination for needy Berlin children.

Schloss Johannisburg

Aschaffenburg, Unterfranken

Schloss Johannisburg prägt mit seinen markanten Treppentürmen bis heute das Stadtbild von Aschaffenburg. Das vom Straßburger Festungsbaumeister Georg Ridinger 1605 bis 1614 aus Rotsandstein in Formen der Renaissance am Mainufer erbaute Schloss ersetzte eine 1552 im Markgräflerkrieg geplünderte und niedergebrannte Burg. Die Johannisburg war die erste Schlossanlage in Deutschland, bei der das Repräsentationsbedürfnis größere Bedeutung bekam als die Funktion als Wehrbau. Der bis Anfang des 19. Jahrhunderts als Zweitsitz der Mainzer Kurfürsten und Erzbischöfe dienende Bau beherbergt heute eine Abteilung der Bayerischen Staatsgemäldesammlung mit bedeutenden Gemälden von Lucas Cranach und Peter Paul Rubens.

Palace Johannisburg shapes the city image of Aschaffenburg even today with its distinctive stair towers. Fortress builder, Georg Ridinger from Straßburg replaced a castle, plundered and burned down in the Margrave Wars in 1552, with a red sandstone palace on the bank of the River Main in the renaissance style from 1605 until 1614. Palace Johannisburg was the first palace estate in Germany in which the representational purpose became more important then its function as a military building. Until the beginning of the 19th century it served as the second seat of the Elector and Arch-bishop of Mainz and today it houses the department of the Bavarian State Painting Collection with distinguished works by Lucas Cranach and Peter Paul Rubens.

Festung Marienberg

Würzburg, Unterfranken

Die Festung Marienberg liegt als Wahrzeichen Würzburgs auf dem Schlossberg hoch über dem Main. In den ältesten Teilen ist die Marienfeste über 1000 Jahre alt. Die über Jahrhunderte als Residenz der Bischöfe dienende Anlage wurde immer wieder umgebaut. Nach Bränden 1572 und 1600 erstand ein zunächst repräsentativer Renaissancebau, nach der Einnahme durch die Schweden im Dreißigjährigen Krieg dann eine barocke Festung, der im 17. Jahrhundert weitere militärische Befestigungen und Bastionen hinzugefügt wurden. Mit der Errichtung der vorgelagerten „Teufelsschanze" und des viergeschossigen Geschützturms an der Südflanke durch Balthasar Neumann, den Erbauer der Würzburger Residenz, erhielt die Marienfeste, in der das Mainfränkische Museum und das Fürstenbaumuseum untergebracht sind, ihr heutiges Gepräge.

The Marienberg fortress is the emblem of Würzburg atop Schlossberg high over the River Main. The oldest sections of the fortress are over 1000 years old. For more than a century, it was the residence of the bishop of Würzburg and was continually rebuilt. Following fires in 1572 and 1600 it was extended to a representative renaissance building. After being taken by the Swedes in the Thirty Years' War, it became a baroque fortress and in the 17th century further military fortifications and bastions were added. With the installation of upstream 'Teufelsschanze' ('devil's entrenchments') and the four-storey protective tower on the southern flank by Balthasar Neumann, the constructor of the residence of Würzburg, fortress Marienberg received its current imprint and today houses the Main-Franconian Museum and the Fürstenbaumuseum.

Würzburger Schloss

Würzburg, Unterfranken

Die Würzburger Residenz zählt zu den bedeutendsten Schlossbauten des europäischen Spätbarock. Über einer rechteckigen Grundfläche als mehrhöfige Anlage von Balthasar Neumann errichtet, besitzt die 167 Meter breite Residenz gewaltige Ausmaße: Der Bau diente bis zur Säkularisation Anfang des 19. Jahrhunderts als Sitz der Würzburger Fürstbischöfe und birgt fast 400 Räume. Trotz der Größe zeichnet er sich durch eine ungewöhnliche Geschlossenheit und Kompaktheit aus. Grandios ist die Raumschöpfung des Treppenhauses, in dem der venezianische Maler Giovanni Battista Tiepolo von 1752 bis 1753 das größte zusammenhängende Deckenfresko überhaupt geschaffen hat. Das Spiegelkabinett des Würzburger Schlosses wurde als das „vollkommenste Raumkunstwerk des Rokoko" bezeichnet. 1981 hat die UNESCO die Würzburger Residenz zum Weltkulturerbe erklärt.

The Residence of Würzburg is among the most prominent palaces of the late-baroque period in Europe. The 167 meter-wide building of sublime proportions sits on a right-angled ground plan with multiple courtyards, built by Balthasar Neumann. The palace served, until its secularization at the beginning of the 19th century, as the seat of the Prince-Bishops of Würzburg and boasts nearly 400 rooms. Despite its size, the building has an exceptional homogeneity and compactness. The use of space in the staircase is another grandiose feature, in which from 1752 to 1753 the Venetian painter, Giovanni Battista Tiepolo created the largest continuous ceiling fresco ever made. The mirror cabinet of the Würzburg Palace has been described as the 'most perfect piece of spatial artwork of the rococo period'. In 1981 UNESCO named the Residence of Würzburg as a World-Heritage Sight.

Veste Irmelshausen

Höchheim, Main-Rhön

Die Anfänge der seit über sechshundert Jahren im Besitz der Herren von Bibra befindlichen und für Touristen nicht zugänglichen Veste Irmelshausen gehen ins Jahr 1376 zurück. Nach Vergrößerungen der Anlage zu Beginn des 16. Jahrhunderts wurden in den Jahren 1556 bis 1561 dem spätgotischen Abschnitt im Nordwesten die drei Flügel des sogenannten „Hansenbaus" hinzugefügt. Die nie zerstörte Anlage besticht mit einem stilistisch abwechslungsreichen Baukörper und zählt, an der Grenze zu Thüringen gelegen, zu den schönsten Wasserschlössern Frankens.

For over 600 years in the possession of the Lords of Bibra, Fortress Irmelshausen dates back to 1376. After enlargements of the estate at the beginning of the 16th century, the late-Gothic three wing portion called 'Hansenbau' was added to the northwest from 1556 to 1561. The never destroyed fortress possesses a stylistic diversified structure that lies on the boarder with Thuringia. It qualifies as one of the most beautiful moated castles of Franconia but is closed to tourists.

Veste Coburg

Coburg, Oberfranken

Die „Fränkische Krone" genannte Veste Coburg bietet herrliche Ausblicke nach Thüringen und Franken. Auf einem nach drei Seiten hin steil abfallenden Bergvorsprung über dem Tal der Itz gelegen, verbindet die im 16. und 17. Jahrhundert zur Landesfestung ausgebaute Burg romanische, gotische und Stilelemente der Renaissance. Ein stellenweise dreifacher Mauerring legt sich um mehrere Innenhöfe: Er machte die Veste, in der bis 1918 die Herzöge von Sachsen-Coburg residierten, uneinnehmbar. In der zwischenzeitlich auch als Zuchthaus, Kranken- und Irrenanstalt eingerichteten Festung wurde 1838 die jetzige Kunstsammlung untergebracht. Die Veste Coburg, in der sich im Jahre 1530 auch Martin Luther aufhielt, ist die zweitgrößte und besterhaltene Burg Deutschlands.

Called the 'Crown of Franconia', Fortress Coburg offers beautiful views of Thuringia and Franconia. It lies on the a steeply sloping mountain jut overlooking Itz Valley. Characteristics of the romanic, gothic, and renaissance style periods are connected together in the fortress, which was expanded in the 16th and 17th centuries. A ring wall, in places threefold, encircles the many interior courtyards and made the fortress, where the Dukes of Sachsen-Coburg resided until 1918, impregnable. The current collection of art housed in the fortress was installed in 1838 after intermittent use also as a penitentiary, hospital, and lunatic asylum. The fortress, in which Martin Luther lived in the year 1530, is the second largest and best-preserved castle in Germany.

Burg Lauenstein

Ludwigsstadt, Oberfranken

Die im thüringisch-fränkischen Schiefergebirge gelegene mittelalterliche Höhenburg Lauenstein in Ludwigsstadt blickt auf eine lange Baugeschichte zurück. Der Palas stammt aus dem 14. Jahrhundert. Im 16. Jahrhundert kamen die anderen Bauteile hinzu, die Burgkapelle und der sogenannte Thüna-Bau, ein mehrgeschossiger prächtiger Trakt mit einem 40 Meter langen kassettengedecken Festsaal. Ende des 19. Jahrhunderts ließ der Burgenromantiker Erhard Messmer die heruntergekommene Burg im Sinne des Späthistorismus und des Jugendstils renovieren und neu ausstatten. Seit 1962 im Besitz der Bayerischen Schlösserverwaltung, beherbergt Burg Lauenstein heute ein Museum und in der Vorburg ein Hotel mit Gartenwirtschaft.

The medieval elevated-fortress Lauenstein in Ludwigsstadt, located in Shale Mountains of Thuringia-Franconia, looks back at a long story of construction. The palace stems from the 14th century. In the 16th century, additional portions were added, including the castle chapel and the 'Thüna-Building', a grand multiple-storey wing with a 40 meter-long Great Hall renovated and newly furnished in the style of the late-historicism and Art Nouveau. Since 1962 it has been in possession of the Bavarian Castle Management Association. Castle Lauenstein currently houses a museum and a hotel with an open-air cafe and restaurant.

Festung Rosenberg

Kronach, Oberfranken

Der Blick aus der Höhe zeigt eine der besterhaltenen und mit 23,6 Hektar eine der größten Festungsanlagen Deutschlands. Die Veste Rosenberg in Kronach verfügt über einen mustergültig angelegten fünfeckigen Befestigungsring, der ein im Laufe von Jahrhunderten entstandenes Bauensemble mit einer viereckigen Kernburg umschließt. Zunächst diente die über der Stadt gelegene Festung als bambergische Bischofsburg, dann als Landesfestung. Ende des 19. Jahrhunderts gelangte die Burg in den Besitz der Stadt. Die Fränkische Galerie, das Frankenwaldmuseum, die jährlichen Faust-Festspiele und andere Einrichtungen machen die Festung Rosenberg zu einem kulturellen Anziehungspunkt der gesamten Region.

The view from above shows one of the most intact and covering 23.6 hectors of land, one of the largest fortresses in Germany. Fortress Rosenberg in Kronach has a pentagon-shaped fortification ring built in an exemplary manner, which surrounds an ensemble of buildings with a central castle on a square shaped ground plan, which stems from different centuries. The fortress, which stands over the city, served as the Bishop of Bamberg's castle and then as a state fortress. At the close of the 19th century the castle fell into the hands of the city of Kronach. The Franconian Gallery, the Franconian Forest Museum, the annual Faust Pageant and other events make Fortress Rosenberg a cultural attraction for the entire region.

Plassenburg

Kulmbach, Oberfranken

Die Plassenburg, das Wahrzeichen der Stadt Kulmbach, ist die bedeutendste Schlossburg der Renaissance in Franken und nimmt unter den Burgen Deutschlands eine herausragende Stellung ein. Die 1135 erstmals erwähnte Festung gehörte von 1338 bis 1791 den Burggrafen von Nürnberg und späteren Markgrafen von Brandenburg aus dem Hause Hohenzollern. Ihre heutige Gestalt als Vierflügelanlage geht auf den Wiederaufbau der im Bundesständischen Krieg zerstörten Burg ab 1559 durch den Kulmbacher Baumeister Caspar Vischer zurück. Der berühmte Arkadenhof bildet mit seinem reichen Reliefdekor einen bemerkenswerten Gegensatz zu den wuchtigen Wehranlagen. Nach diversen Nutzungen als Lazarett, Zuchthaus und Kriegsgefangenenlager beherbergt die Plassenburg heute das Deutsche Zinnfigurenmuseum, die Staatlichen Museen Plassenburg sowie das Landschaftsmuseum Obermain. Im Arkadenhof finden kulturelle Veranstaltungen statt. Die Schlosskirche wird für Gottesdienste, Trauungen, Taufen und Konzerte genutzt.

The Plassenburg, the landmark of the city of Kulmbach, is the most significant renaissance castle in Franconia and takes a prominent place among all of Germany's castles. First mentioned in 1135, the fortress belonged to the Burgraves of Nürnberg, the later Margraves of Brandenburg from the House of Hohenzollern. Its current form as a four-winged-estate goes back to its rebuilding after destruction in the War of the Bundesstände under the direction of master builder Caspar Vischer of Kulmbach following 1559. The well-known arcade courtyard, with its rich relief décor, creates a remarkable contrast to the weighty military facilities. After its diverse usage as military hospital, penitentiary, and prisoner of war camp, Plassenburg now houses the 'German Museum of Pewter Figures', the State Museums of Plassenburg, as well as the Landscape Museum of the Upper-Main. Cultural programs take place in the arcade courtyard. The palace church is now used for church services, weddings, baptisms, and concerts.

Giechburg

Scheßlitz, Oberfranken

Die bereits 1125 urkundlich erwähnte Giechburg in Scheßlitz im Landkreis Bamberg diente seit Ende des 14. Jahrhunderts als Bamberger Amtsburg. Im Hussitenkrieg, im Deutschen Bauernkrieg und im sogenannten Markgrafenkrieg wurde die Burg erheblich beschädigt. Bei der Neugestaltung der Anlage Anfang des 17. Jahrhunderts war nur der Burgfried aus dem 13. Jahrhundert erhalten. Neu entstanden die um den Hof gruppierten Wohngebäude und die Ringmauer mit den Türmen und Bastionen, die die Burg den Dreißigjährigen Krieg unbeschadet überstehen ließ. 1808 verwandelte der bayerische Landbauinspektor von Hohenhausen die Burg Giebich nach dem Geschmack der Zeit in eine „malerische Ruine". Als neuer Eigentümer machte der Landkreis Bamberg 1974 die unterdessen zerfallene Giechburg wieder zu einer touristischen Attraktion.

Giechburg in Scheßlitz, located in the Bamberg region, was first documented in 1125. Since the end of the 14th century it served as an administrative seat of the Archbishop of Bamberg. During the Hussite Wars as well as during the German Peasants' War and during the so called Margrave War the castle received considerable damage. Only the 13th century donjon was left when the castle at the beginning of the 17th century was constructed. Newly constructed were a group of residential rooms grouped around the courtyard and a ring wall with towers and bastions which survived irrespective of the Thirty Years' War. In 1808 the Bavarian country building inspector, von Hohenhausen, transformed the Castle Giebich into a 'picturesque ruin', which was the fashion of the time. As the new owners, the region of Bamberg made time-decayed Giechburg again into a tourist attraction.

Schloss Seehof

Memmelsdorf bei Bamberg, Oberfranken

Mit seinen markanten Ecktürmen und imposanten Kuppeldachhauben zählt der massige Vierflügelbau von Schloss Seehof in Memmelsdorf zu den eindrucksvollsten Schlossanlagen des deutschen Barock. Dabei befand sich die 1686 nach Plänen von Antonio Petrini errichtete Sommerresidenz der Bamberger Fürstbischöfe noch Ende des 20. Jahrhunderts in einem desolaten Zustand, der umfangreiche Sanierungsmaßnahmen erforderlich machte. Vom einstigen Reichtum des Rokokogartens haben sich einige Sandsteinskulpturen von Ferdinand Tietz und eine restaurierte Kaskade mit Wasserspielen erhalten. Sehenswert ist auch der „Weiße Saal" mit einem grandiosen Deckengemälde von Giuseppe Appiani. Heute beherbergt der ehemalige Herrensitz das Bayerische Landesamt für Denkmalpflege.

With its distinctive corner towers and imposing roof-bonnets, the massive four-winged structure of Palace Seehof in Memmelsdorf qualifies as one of the most impressive palace constructions of the German baroque period. It was constructed as a summer residence for the Prince-Bishop of Bamberg from plans by Antonio Petrini in 1686, but could only be found in desolate condition at the end of the 20th century, making extensive restoration measures necessary. A few of Ferdinand Tietz' sandstone sculptures and a cascade with trick fountains give hints to the former opulence of its rococo gardens. Also worth seeing is the 'Weißer Saal' ('white hall') with a grandiose ceiling fresco by Giuseppe Appiani. Today the former manor accommodates the Bavarian State Authorities for the Protection of Historic Buildings.

Schloss Nymphenburg

München

Schloss Nymphenburg wurde als Sommerresidenz der Bayerischen Kurfürsten im Westen Münchens errichtet. Den Auftakt der Bautätigkeit bildete 1664 bis 1674 der kubische Mitteltrakt mit Freitreppe von den Münchner Hofbaumeistern Agostino Barelli und Enrico Zuccalli. Dem formal zurückhaltenden Bau wurden Anfang des 18. Jahrhunderts nach Plänen von Zuccalli und Joseph Effner die Galerien, die vier Pavillons sowie Marstall, Orangerie und „Kloster" hinzugefügt. Zur Stadt hin schließt ein halbkreisförmiges Rondell die weitläufige barocke Anlage. Mit seiner prachtvollen Ausstattung und dem bedeutenden Park zählt Schloss Nymphenburg zu den größten Sehenswürdigkeiten Münchens.

Nymphenburg Palace was erected to the west of Munich as the summer residence of the Bavarian elector. Master builders of the Court, Agostino Barelli and Enrico Zuccalli of Munich constructed the cubic middle section with its exterior stair as the initial activity of construction from 1664 to 1674. The galleries, four pavilions, as well as the stables, orangery, and the 'cloister' were added to the formally reserved building in the beginning of the 18th century according to the designs of Zuccalli und Joseph Effner. A large-scale semicircular rondel encloses the far-reaching estate facing toward the city. With its grandiose configuration and the superior park, Nymphenburg Palace belongs to the list of the most beautiful sights of Munich.

Schloss Herrenchiemsee

Herrenchiemsee, Chiemsee/Bayern

Schloss Herrenchiemsee war das letzte große Bauprojekt Ludwigs II. (1845–1886). Obwohl das auf der Insel Herrenchiemsee im Chiemsee zwischen 1878 und 1886 erbaute Schloss lediglich für private Zwecke und als persönliches Refugium gedacht war, wählte sich der kapriziöse Bayernkönig ausgerechnet Versailles als Vorbild, den Regierungssitz der französischen Könige. Zwanzig Prunkräume, darunter die Gesandtentreppe, die famose Spiegelgalerie und das Paradeschlafzimmer, wurden realisiert. Dann wurde der Weiterbau aus Geldmangel eingestellt. Nach dem Tode Ludwigs kam es sogar zum Rückbau einzelner Bauabschnitte. So blieb es bei einem dreiflügeligen Haupttrakt in einem prachtvollen Schlosspark, der nach Plänen von Carl von Effner ebenfalls dem Versailler Vorbild folgt.

Palace Herrenchiemsee was the great final building project of Ludwig II (1845–1886). The palace was built between 1878 and 1886 only for private purposes and was thought of as a type of refuge on the island Herrenchiemsee in the Chiemsee. Nevertheless, the capricious Bavarian king considered Versailles, the governmental seat of the King of France, to be its archetype. Twenty pompous showrooms, the 'Gesandtentreppe' (a copy of Versailles' 'Ambassador's Staircase'), the famous 'Great Hall of Mirrors', and the Parade Bedroom were all realized before further building was discontinued due to a lack of funds. After Ludwig's death, some parts of the building were actually dismantled. Today remains the three-wing main estate in the middle of the magnificent palace gardens, that were based on Carl von Effner's plans, which exactly followed the model of Versailles likewise.

Schloss Neuschwanstein

Schwangau bei Füssen, Allgäu

Auf einem Felsen in der unvergleichlichen Bergszenerie um Alp- und Schwansee gelegen, gehört Schloss Neuschwanstein zu den bekanntesten Touristenzielen Deutschlands. 1,3 Millionen Gäste jährlich besuchen diesen Inbegriff deutscher Romantik. König Ludwig II. wünschte ein Schloss „im echten Styl der alten deutschen Ritterburgen" und beauftragte mit dem Bauentwurf den Bühnenmaler Christian Jank. Dabei ist Neuschwanstein keine Wiederholung einer mittelalterlichen Burganlage, sondern eine Neuschöpfung aus dem Geist des Historismus und des Eklektizismus des 19. Jahrhunderts. Nach den Vorstellungen Ludwigs, der sich zur Zeit seiner Entmündigung hier aufhielt, sollte das Schloss den Gedanken des Königtums von Gottes Gnaden symbolisieren.

Atop a crag situated in the incomparable mountain scenery surrounding Alpsee and Schwansee, Palace Neuschwanstein is one of Germany's most well-known tourist destinations. Each year 1.3 million guests visit this embodiment of German Romanticism. King Ludwig II desired his palace to be 'in the authentic style of the old German knights' castles' and commissioned the stage painter Christian Jank for the structural design. However, Neuschwanstein is no repetition of any medieval castle layout, but rather a new creation in the spirit of the historicism and eclecticism, which ruled the style discussion in the 19th century. Ludwig lived in Neuschwanstein at the time when he was incapacitated. According to his suggestion, the palace was to symbolize and bring to mind a kingdom of God's grace.

Adressen

Schloss Glücksburg
Große Straße
24960 Glücksburg

Schloss Gottorf
24837 Schleswig

Gut Emkendorf
Gutshof 3
24802 Emkendorf

Blomenburg
Blomenburger Allee
24238 Selent

Schloss Plön
24306 Plön

Gut Salzau
24256 Salzau

Schloss Eutin
Schlossplatz 5
23701 Eutin

Schloss Tremsbüttel
Schlossstr. 10
22967 Tremsbüttel

Schloss Ahrensburg
Lübecker Str. 1
22926 Ahrensburg

Schloss Celle
Schlossplatz 1
29221 Celle

Schloss Gifhorn
Schlossplatz 1
38518 Gifhorn

Schloss Wolfsburg
Schlossstr. 8
38448 Wolfsburg

Schloss Schwerin
Lennéstr. 1
19053 Schwerin

Schloss Ludwigslust
Schlossfreiheit
19288 Ludwigslust

Schlosshotel Boitzenburg
Templiner Str. 13
17268 Boitzenburger Land

Schloss Rheinsberg
Mühlenstr. 1
16829 Rheinsberg

Schloss Liebenberg
Ortsteil Liebenberg
16775 Löwenberger Land

Schlossmuseum Oranienburg
Schlossplatz 2
16501 Oranienburg

Schloss Charlottenburg
Luisenplatz
10585 Berlin

Schloss Bellevue
Spreeweg 1
10557 Berlin-Tiergarten

Schloss und Park Sanssouci
Maulbeerallee
14469 Potsdam

Schloss und Park Babelsberg
Park Babelsberg 11
14482 Potsdam

Schloss Neuhardenberg
Schinkelplatz
15320 Neuhardenberg

Schloss und Park Branitz
Robinienweg 5
03042 Cottbus

Albrechtsburg
Domplatz
01662 Meißen

Schloss Moritzburg
Schlossallee 3 B
01468 Moritzburg

Zwinger
Theaterplatz 1
01067 Dresden

Schloss Pillnitz
August-Böckstiegel-Str. 2
01326 Dresden

Schloss Rammenau
01877 Rammenau

Festung Königstein
01824 Königstein

Schloss Augustusburg
09573 Augustusburg/Sachsen

Burg Scharfenstein
Schlossberg 1
09135 Scharfenstein

Schloss Quedlinburg
06484 Quedlinburg

Wartburg
Auf der Wartburg
99817 Eisenach

Schloss Augustusburg
Schlossstr. 6
50321 Brühl

Schloss Arenfels
53557 Bad Hönningen

Schloss Stolzenfels
56075 Koblenz

Marksburg
56338 Braubach

Burg Sterrenberg
56341 Kamp-Bornhofen

Burg Liebenstein
56341 Kamp-Bornhofen

Burg Maus
Bachstr. 30b
56346 St. Goarshausen-Wellmich

Burg Stahleck
55422 Bacharach

Burg Ehrenfels am Rhein
nordwestlich von Rüdesheim (Hessen)

Schloss Saarbrücken
Schlossplatz
66119 Saarbrücken

Schloss Heidelberg
Schlosshof 1
69117 Heidelberg

Schloss Schwetzingen
68723 Schwetzingen

Schloss Ludwigsburg
Schlossstr. 30
71634 Ludwigsburg

Neues Schloss
Schlossplatz 4
70173 Stuttgart

Burg Hohenzollern
72379 Burg Hohenzollern
Gemarkung Bisingen

Schloss Johannisburg
Schlossplatz 4
63739 Aschaffenburg

Festung Marienberg
97082 Würzburg

Residenz und Hofgarten Würzburg
Residenzplatz 2
97070 Würzburg

Veste Irmelshausen
97633 Höchheim

Veste Coburg
96450 Coburg

Burg Lauenstein
Burgstraße 3
96337 Ludwigsstadt

Festung Rosenberg
96317 Kronach

Plassenburg
95326 Kulmbach

Giechburg
Giechburg 1
96110 Scheßlitz

Schloss und Park Seehof
96117 Memmelsdorf

Schloss und Park Nymphenburg
80638 München

Neues Schloss und Park Herrenchiemsee
83209 Herrenchiemsee

Schloss Neuschwanstein
Neuschwansteinstr. 20
87645 Schwangau

© 2008 Nicolaische Verlagsbuchhandlung GmbH, Berlin

Fotografien: Dirk Laubner
Texte: Andreas Denk, Bonn/Berlin; PD Dr. Britta-Juliane Kruse, Berlin;
Alice Sàrosi, Bonn; Dr. Martin Seidel, Bonn
Übersetzung: Alissa Burmeister, Berlin
Redaktion: Andreas Denk, PD Dr. Britta-Juliane Kruse
Layoutgestaltung: Jo.Seibt Kommunikationsdesign, Leverkusen
Umschlaggestaltung: Jonas Maron, Berlin
Reproduktion: PPP, Köln
Druck: Rasch Druck, Bramsche
Bindung: Bramscher Buchbinder Betriebe, Bramsche

ISBN 978-3-89479-360-9

Unter **www.nicolai-verlag.de** können Sie unseren Newsletter abonnieren, der Sie über
das Programm und aktuelle Neuerscheinungen des Nicolai Verlags informiert.